Handling
Problem
Volunteers

Sue Vineyard &
Steve McCurley

Handling Problem Volunteers

Other Books by the Authors:

Books by Vineyard and McCurley:

101 Ideas for Volunteer Programs
101 Ways to Raise Resources
101 Tips for Volunteer Recruitment
101 MORE Ideas for Volunteer Programs
Managing Volunteer Diversity: A Rainbow of Opportunity
Measuring UP! Assessment Tools for Volunteer Programs
&
GRAPEVINE: Volunteerism's Newsletter.

Books by Steve McCurley:

Recruiting Volunteers for Difficult & Long Term Assignments
Volunteer Management: Mobilizing All The Resources of the Community

Books by Sue Vineyard:

Beyond Banquets, Plaques & Pins: Creative Ways to Recognize Volunteers
Marketing Magic for Volunteer Programs
How to Take Care of You So You Can Take Care of Others
Evaluating Volunteers, Programs & Events
Secrets of Leadership
Secrets of Motivation: How to Get and Keep Volunteers & Paid Staff
The Great Trainers Guide: How to Train (almost) Anyone to do (almost) Anything!
Megatrends & Volunteerism: Mapping the Future of Volunteer Programs
Stop Managing Volunteers! New Competencies for Volunteer Administrators

Published by:
Heritage Arts Publishing
VMSystems
1807 Prairie Avenue
Downers Grove, IL 60515

Sales & Distribution: 800/272-8306
Editorial Office: 630/964-1194
FAX: 630/964-7338

Table of Contents

Chapter One
Introduction

Myths about Problem Volunteers

There are myths that surround problem volunteers, and when accepted as truths, they impede a healthy climate in an organization. This, in turn, causes many good volunteers to leave a program, results in potential volunteers who hear horror stories about problems to decide to volunteer elsewhere and causes paid staff to lose confidence in working partnerships with volunteers.

Volunteer managers cannot afford to hang on to any of the following myths or allow volunteer leaders within their program to do so. Some of these myths include:

1. *"Ignoring problems will make they go away."* WRONG. They may go underground and be harder to identify but they won't go away!

2. *"No one else notices."* Don't fool yourself into martyrdom. Thinking that you alone are suffering with a volunteer who constantly complains is foolish. If the volunteer complains to you about others, she probably complains to others about you!

3. *"I can fix a dysfunctional person."* Wrong again. That's not in the job description of volunteer managers. Trying to do so will drain energies, reduce creativity and probably cause the 98% of volunteers who are not troublesome to lose patience with their manager's priorities and decisiveness. Volunteer managers must address problems and consequences caused by people in their program but they really can't FIX a truly dysfunctional person.

4. *"There's good in everyone...we just need to give them time to show it."* Here is where people can get bogged down in philosophical debates, but for the purpose of this book we need to admit that there are some nasty people with less-than-honorable reasons to volunteer. Giving a pedophile "time" to see the error of his ways is not in the job description of any volunteer director. Allowing someone who delights in starting rumors that are deeply destructive to clients, staff and other volunteers is NOT in the best interest of the program. As difficult as it may be to admit, there are some bad seeds around.

5. *"A confrontation will make things worse. They might get mad."* That may be true for a short time, but NOT confronting will make matters worse for sure. If having someone angry is a terrifying thought, it might be good to get some counseling in assertiveness. The volunteer manager must keep control and remain focused on the overall good of the program and its effectiveness.

6. *"A confrontation might result in the volunteer leaving and if they do, the program will fall apart."* If that is correct, and a program is that dependent on the presence of a single person, there are problems much deeper than a conflict with one person. Such a program leader needs immediate help.

7. *"If I'm truly a caring person, I can handle all the people who are problems."* Get over the myth that a volunteer manager has to be a saint. Never believe press clippings - a graduate degree from the School of Nicey-Nice is not necessarily a good thing. All the caring in the world won't solve the problems caused by nasty, spoiled, dominating trouble-makers.

8. *"Everyone wants to be fixed."* Not true. There are some people who actually enjoy their dysfunction. Some whiners like to whine. Some people who are rude and bossy get a kick out of that behavior. Some chronically dependent people like that role because it forces others to rescue them and actually makes them dominant!

There are even some highly dysfunctional people to whom failure is success. Their goal is to be a victim when things go wrong or people get angry at them. Being a victim is their way of getting sympathy from on-lookers, soothing "now, now dear" statements from rescuers and full blown pity-parties from all the mother-superiors in a five mile area. No, everyone does NOT want to be fixed!

When any of the above myths persist, much

time and energy is wasted as people try to circumvent the unresolved conflicts such false beliefs create. At all costs, reject these myths. The ultimate task of a manager is to work with others, both the good and the bad. As a volunteer manager most of the people you encounter will be among the most productive and rewarding workers that exist; some, however, will be exceptions to the rule. Your job as a manager is to deal with both types, encouraging the efforts of one and correcting the efforts of the other. Denial of the problem, unfortunately, is not an option.

About This Book

This book is designed to help you handle a variety of problem volunteers. We have divided its coverage in increasing depths of seriousness, from the annoying to the disruptive to the totally dysfunctional.

Each chapter begins with the discussion of some specific problem types, followed by suggestions on how to deal with them, and then concludes with some general suggestions that apply to all of the situations covered in the chapter.

The final chapters provide some additional materials and references that you may find helpful.

Chapter Two
Analyzing the Situation

Introduction
The first thing to do when dealing with a problem volunteer is to determine what is really going on. Part of this is determining the extent of the problem situation (and, indeed, whether there really is a *problem*), but the more crucial element involves attempting to determine the root cause of the problem.

Detecting Impending Problems
There are some common warning signs that indicate approaching problems in workers, paid or volunteer. A combination of these calls for a re-interview with the person and/or a re-examination of the job assignment to uncover what is behind the behavior. Warning signs include:

1. The quality and quantity of work begins to decline. The worker makes many mistakes.

2. The worker often comes late to assignments.

3. The volunteer simply does not show up for work or meetings.

4. There is a palatable lack of enthusiasm.

5. Rarely, if ever, does the worker make suggestions or show initiative.

6. A normally verbal and open volunteer or employee becomes silent and closed-down.

7. The worker continues to avoid parts of their job--especially those that are more complex or disagreeable to them.

8. Workers blame others for their own errors or short comings.

9. They are less agreeable, affable or cooperative; they whine or complain regularly.

10. They avoid interaction with colleagues; they make sure they are unavailable for any social interaction.

11. They ignore timelines and due dates for projects.

12. Co-workers and direct supervisors complain about the worker and their performance.

13. Reports reach volunteer managers of the worker "bad-mouthing" the organization, program or key leaders.

14. They explode over insignificant instances; reactions are out of proportion to incidents.

15. They project an attitude of "nothing is right."

Finding Out What is Really Happening
Consider the demonstration of any of these behaviors a warning that something is wrong; a combination of several of these needs to be seen as symptomatic of a serious underlying problem. Take one or more of the following steps and responses:

1. Meet in private with the person. Describe what specifically has been observed and ask them if there is an underlying issue that needs to be discussed. Do not place any interpretation on the observed behavior; allow them to explain it if they will.

2. Avoid rushing to judgment of the feedback that is being given. Listen attentively, do not interrupt and allow silent spaces in the conversation that can allow them time to gather their thoughts and consider how to express themselves. Encourage honest feedback through body language, attentive listening and avoidance of defensiveness.

3. Determine the real issues motivating behavior:

- Has something changed in their personal

life that is forcing a shift in priorities, energy allocation, concentration, etc.? A critically ill child at home can distract a typically enthusiastic volunteer and cause many of the problem symptoms noted here.

- Are they the victims of mis-information? Do they believe as a paid worker that they are to be replaced by a volunteer? Certainly that could cause a lessened amount of cooperation!

- Are they upset about a specific occurrence and thus "fighting back" by reducing their productivity?

- Have they simply burned out? Volunteers, like paid workers, can stay in a job or location beyond their energy limits. We'll talk about this more in our next chapter.

4.   Ask the volunteer or staff member what they see as a successful response to their issues. What would be best for them? A time-out or leave-of-absence to regain their old enthusiasm? A move to a different assignment? A full release from the perceived burden of staying?

5.   Agree on a time frame for the resolution of the problem. If leaving is the chosen option, select the time frame best for the program. Allowing a disgruntled volunteer to stay for a month when the volunteer manager feels they will continue to contaminate the work climate is unwise even in the face of the volunteer's assurances that they'll be positive and productive.

When behavior becomes abnormal or negative, consider the actions as symptoms and warnings of problems about to erupt and take steps to intervene swiftly. Remember that the "problem" may be the person involved, but it might also be the situation that exists or the relationship among several persons that is the root cause.

Questions to Determine Problem Behavior

Very often, particularly in minor problem behavior, there will be no real "villain." Two people in the organization might just be not getting along, or they may even have a simple misunderstanding in which neither is really at fault. These innocent situations often create larger difficulties, however, if unaddressed. A

good volunteer manager can sometimes intervene and assist the parties to look for their own solution to the situation before things get out of hand. The best process for attempting this involves talking with the parties involved on an individual basis and getting them to describe their version of the difficulty as well as what they think they could do to address the problem. Note that the solution offered here is not for the volunteer manager to act to solve the problem, but rather to encourage and assist the involved parties to identify what they themselves can do to resolve the difficulty.

The following are some good questions to use during the interview with a problem volunteer. They are grouped into examining the background of the situation (including how the problem volunteer feels about what is happening), creating possible solution options, and  creating an implementation plan for helping the problem volunteer address the situation:

1.   *Background Investigation*

✓ How are things going?
✓ Why do you think they are going so well?
✓ How could things be better?
✓ What problems are you having?
✓ Why are those problems happening?
✓ What factors in the situation caused the problems?
✓ Are the difficulties related to a single person or to most persons?
✓ How long has the situation been this way?
✓ What happened prior to this situation?
✓ Is there a time when this seems most likely to occur?
✓ Does this behavior happen with everybody or only with some people?
✓ What problems does this person's behavior cause?
✓ Why do you think the person behaves that

way?
✓ What would a person get out of behaving that way?
✓ How are other staff and volunteers reacting to the behavior?
✓ Have you talked with the person about the behavior?
✓ What was the person's reaction when you talked with them?

2 *Creation of Options*

✓ What do you think you might do if the situation/behavior doesn't change?
✓ What has been your response?
✓ What has been the person's reaction to your response?
✓ Why do you think this response didn't work?
✓ Are there other responses you might consider?
✓ How do you suppose the person will react to these?
✓ What are the pro's and con's of that course?
✓ What other options do we have?
✓ If you had it to do over again, what would you do differently?
✓ What would you advise someone else to do in this situation?
✓ What would you advise someone else to do to avoid this situation?

3. *Implementation*

✓ Of the possible options, which would best fit with your situation?
✓ What will you need before trying to implement the solution?
✓ How will this affect other volunteers and staff in your department?
✓ Is there a way to best communicate this change to these others?
✓ Are there any advantages to the way we now do things that we want to preserve?
✓ How will you monitor responses to this attempted solution?
✓ Is there anything I can do to help make your plan work?

✓ When can we talk about this again?

Analyzing Behavior

We'd like to offer two processes you might use in thinking through a problem situation. The first is a question-path to suggest how to deal with a problem situation, such as a deficiency in knowledge or performance.

You can see the question-path below. You will note that it is designed to help you "coach" the problem volunteer, allowing you to determine how the problem situation might best be approached. It offers a logical way of thinking through your options, and is applicable to a wide range of problem situations. Simply follow the arrows to see the recommended action.

You begin in the upper left hand corner by describing the problem situation and its consequences. You then ask yourself if the consequences matter, that is if they are substantial enough and detrimental enough to warrant attention.

Coaching Analysis

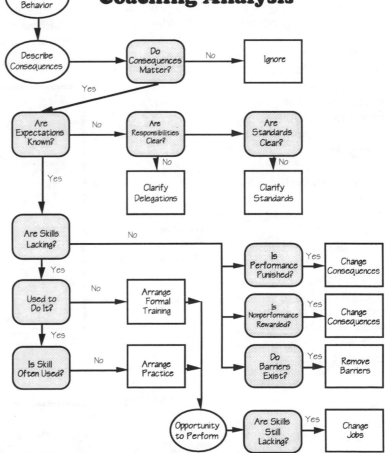

If the answer is "no," your best action is to do nothing. If the answer is "yes," then you proceed to determining whether the volunteer understands the expectations, responsibilities and standards of the position.

If these are not the source of the problem, then you examine a decision-tree involving the skills needed to perform the work, leading eventually to the possibility of training.

If the problem is one of attitude toward the job then you can examine whether the consequences of poor behavior have been adequately explained and applied in this situation.

While a seemingly simple tool, this process may help you in examining all the possible alternatives in analyzing problem behavior.

A second process for evaluating problem behavior was originally developed by Rick Lynch. It consists of a performance analysis chart in which the manager evaluates the employee based on their ability to perform the work and their interest in performing the work.

On the left side of the chart, the manager evaluates the knowledge held by the volunteer, indicating their possession of the skills and ability necessary to do the job. This rating is given on a 1 to 10 scale, with 10 being the high rating. A horizontal line is then drawn across the chart at this rating point.

On the lower side of the chart, the manager evaluates the volunteer in terms of their attitude about the job, whether they have the willingness to perform this type of work. A vertical line is then drawn across the chart at this rating point. The intersection of the two lines may indicate what type of remedial action is

appropriate.

If, for example, you rated a problem volunteer as having a attitudinal desire to do the work (a "7," for example) but also rated them as deficient in knowledge about the work (a "3", for example), then the intersection of these two lines would fall into the quadrant of the performance analysis chart which suggests that "training" is the way to address this performance problem - the volunteer is willing to do the work, but just doesn't know how.

Similarly, a volunteer rated as high in knowledge but low in attitude would probably be one who needed to be re-motivated. A volunteer rated high in knowledge and high in attitude, but who still was not performing satisfactorily is probably an individual who is being preventing from working effectively due to some outside influence or a lack of appropriate resources.

A volunteer who rates low in both knowledge and attitude is one who is either in the wrong job or the wrong organization.

Why Volunteers May Fail to Perform

There are a number of possible reasons to examine and consider when attempting to identify why a volunteer might not be performing as

Performance Analysis Chart

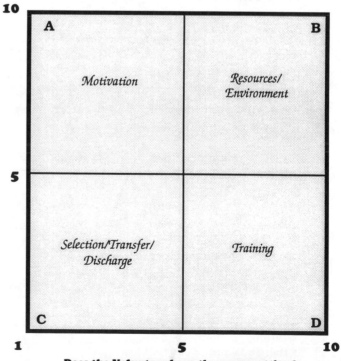

Does the Volunteer have adequate knowledge to perform the job?

Does the Volunteer have the proper attitude (desire) to perform the job?

expected. They include:

- The volunteer is not really motivated to do the work in the first place, or has lost motivation over time.

- The volunteer does not know what they should do or how they should be doing it.

- The volunteer does not understand or agree with the reason for doing the work or doing it the way that you believe it should be done.

- The volunteer has not been consulted in the nature of the work assigned to them and resents this fact.

- There are no incentives for the volunteer to perform to standard and no negative consequences for poor performance.

- The volunteer thinks their performance is at an acceptable level.

- There are other obstacles or other people preventing the volunteer from performing.

- The volunteer has other concerns which are considered more important than performing the work.

- The volunteer is deriving some sense of satisfaction out of the misperformance.

Each of these should be considered in attempting to analyze the performance problem.

Is It A Problem Person or A Problem Climate?

Sometimes a volunteer program that is experiencing an inordinate number of conflicts may have a problem that goes deeper than the people involved. Just as a manager must uncover the real issues in a conflict, so must

they look deeper if there is a pattern of discord among many different people. Is the problem really the people or is it coming from some other cause?

One deeper issue that deserves a close examination in a conflict-ridden organization is the climate within its walls.

The climate is the overall setting in an organization; it is the "feel" of the workplace and is determined by the norms or unwritten rules of behavior that exist. Norms center around procedures, communication, friendliness, ethics, access to information, relationships, clarity of purpose or assignments.

They determine how energy is spent, how pleasurable it is to work there and how growth is encouraged:

- If available energy can be spent accomplishing the goals of the agency, people feel productive and good and tend to work well together; if, however, energy must be spent on trying to survive, figuring out what needs to be done or working around unresolved conflicts, prima-donnas and murky communication, people will be less likely to be productive or stay on as a volunteer.

- If relationships are frowned upon between workers or categories of workers, it will seem less "friendly" to work there and trust will not be established, resulting in suspicions, turf issues and direct conflict.

- If appropriate "fun" and freedom are discouraged, volunteers will not stay too long. Life is hectic and stress-ridden enough, without adding more of the same in volunteer work assignments. Keep in mind that people spend their time and energy where it is most rewarded, offers the best return and provides the greatest satisfaction. Who would want to work in a setting where no one is friendly, no fun is allowed and available energies must be spent on just trying to survive?

Handling Problem Volunteers

To assess their climate, volunteer managers will need to identify existing norms with the input of several perspectives such as volunteers, paid staff, hierarchy, middle-management, board members, supporters, etc. Establish a atmosphere of trust and confidentiality in the discussions that focus on issues not people; keep participants on track, record specifics and do not allow anyone to "shoot down" another's feelings and perspectives. Look both at the unwritten rules that govern behavior, called "norms" and those "SUPER-norms" which are behavior rules that have grown so strong they have been turned into written mandates.

Keep in mind that some rules are beyond debate - they may be mandated by higher authorities such as rules around handling of bodily fluids to protect people from blood-born pathogens in health care facilities.

The purpose of a discussion of norms is to separate positives and negatives. In this discussion:

1. Identify norms and rules; categorize them into non-negotiable (mandates) and negotiable (non-mandates).

2. Examine assumptions people might have about any norms or actions that may seem non-negotiable but in fact are not. Look especially at what some consider "sacred cows," those things that have gone on for years such as the Holiday Bach Concert that everyone hates but thinks is untouchable. Maybe it's time to nudge Bach out of his favored spotlight and do something that won't cause as much resentment!

3. Look at the list of non-negotiable factors in your setting. If they are a source of conflict, how can that irritation be reduced? Can the length of time or exposure a volunteer has to this factor be reduced? Is there something that would make a mundane or boring assignment take on new significance? Stuffing envelopes is awful if a sole volunteer is given 5000 to do at home but a "stuffing party and potluck" of 10 volunteers becomes fun. How can the "must" work be re-configured to cause less conflict and more satisfaction?

4. Look at the list of norms categorized as non-mandated. Are there norms that govern how people come on time to work? Their reliability? How volunteers and staff work together? How relationships are encouraged or discouraged?

Divide norms into positive or negative, being careful to offer specific examples of the consequences of each category. Identify those norms that have some positive and some negative aspects. Use creative problem solving to find ways to encourage and strengthen the positives and reduce or eliminate the negatives.

5. Examine how the organization enforces the norms - gently or harshly? If, in a program that prides itself on people coming to work on time, a new volunteer shows up late, how will the positive "on time" norm be projected to them? Will a supervisor chide them for being late, put them down, attack them for tardiness or will they be informed that there is concerted effort to come on time and accept responsibility for not conveying this to them properly? It's the difference between the warm fuzzy approach and the cold prickly!

Positive climates enable people to put their energies into accomplishing the goals and vision of the organization and is characterized by a sense of trust among workers, paid and non-paid. The climate sets the tone for what is accomplished and how people feel while working there. This in turn determines their length of stay, their productivity and what they tell others, a form of personal recruiting.

When conflicts seem to be popping up regularly between workers in an organization, it is wise to look to its root cause. Often it is discovered that the problem is not the people but the climate in which they work.

Not Becoming Part of the Problem Yourself

It is critical not to become a contributing part of the problem, something which is easier to do than you may think.

Managers will often avoid dealing with problem volunteers, for several reasons:

1. You may not want to admit that you have a problem volunteer because you think it reflects badly on you and your supervisory skill.

2. You don't want to confront the volunteer because you're too nice and you think that as a volunteer they should be allowed some latitude.

3. You're friends with the volunteer and don't want to appear to be criticizing them.

4. You're wrapped up in your own work and don't need any more problems to deal with.

5. You may feel sorry for the volunteer, feeling that the lack of performance is not really their fault.

Avoiding problems seldom eliminates them, and usually allows them to build into more complex and troublesome situations. Being a manager means being willing to deal with managerial problems.

You can also become part of the problem by how you approach a problem situation. Here are some common ways for a manager to exacerbate a problem situation:

- *Overreacting*. Some managers explode at petty situations, lashing out at others, especially when they are harboring some resentment for past transgressions.

- *Whining*. Some managers will spend their time complaining to others about the problem rather than directly dealing with the person involved.

- *Lecturing*. Some managers will treat offenders as though they were children, lecturing to them rather than talking with them. This technique doesn't even work very well with children.

- *Nuking*. Some managers avoid confronting problems until they unleash a massive retaliatory strike, annihilating everyone in their path.

Probably the prime sin that a manager can have is laziness, which in the case of problem volunteers often results in lax

interviewing and screening processes, which allows the problem person into the volunteer program in the first place. Always remember that interviewing is the key quality control element in volunteer management.

The steps we've outlined earlier in this chapter advocate a calmer, more rational, and more progressive approach. They view the manager as a coach and consultant to volunteers, recognizing that none of us are perfect, all of us have and cause problems occasionally, and most of us are amendable to improvement if we are approached in the right way.

Chapter Three
The Somewhat Annoying Volunteer

Introduction
The most common types of problem volunteers are people whose interpersonal relations skills leave something to be desired. In this chapter we examine some situations which involve problems of this type and offer suggestions on supervisory techniques which will help in redirecting the actions of the volunteer.

The Hypercritical Volunteer
In addressing problems within a program, the volunteer manager will invariably encounter volunteers and paid staff who offer criticism of their decisions or actions.

In such cases the manager must respond in a way that does not make the conflict worse or widen an already existing gap in the cooperation level between themselves and the accuser.

The following are six possible responses to criticism suggested by Elaine Yarbrough, Ph.D. in her highly acclaimed monograph *Constructive Conflict*. Remember, the goal is to define the conflict so one can begin to understand the concerns of the other. When this is accomplished a real dialogue can begin to facilitate work on real issues.

Sue, the volunteer manager, is confronted by Carol, a long term volunteer who angrily states: "You never listen to my advice; you act as if I have nothing of value to offer."

In response, Sue can choose to do any of the following:

1. Seek more information:

- Ask for specifics: "*Can you give me an example to help me better understand your point?*"
- Guess about specifics: "*Are you referring to the last board meeting when I did not vote to hold the new fund raiser you proposed?*"
- Paraphrase the speaker's ideas: "*It sounds as though you're upset because you think I don't respect your opinions.*"

2. Agree with the speaker:

- Agree with the facts: "*You're right, I don't listen enough to all your suggestions, especially when I'm the most rushed and weary.*"
- Agree with the perception: "*I can see how you might think I'm not listening to your suggestions. Let me tell you how I perceive our interactions.*"

3. Make reassuring comments:

- Problem-focused reassurance: "*I'm certain we can work this problem out.*"
- Relationship-focused reassurance: "*I care about our relationship and I know you do too. We'll find a way to work well together.*"
- Fear-focused reassurance: "*I sense you are frightened about my respect for your opinion and I want to assure you I have the highest respect for all you offer as suggestions.*" (Use this only when the other has expressed their fear; avoid any assumptions.)

4. Role-take:

- Ask the other to take your position: "*What do you think I think?*" "*What do you see happening if I did as you wished?*"
- Take the other's position: "*From your perspective, I would probably think the same as you do.*"

5. Slow down the process:

- Talk more slowly.
- Pause before responding.
- Take a time out, get coffee, suggest a meeting the next day, etc.
- Write down what the other is saying so you can clarify the issues and what the other

might be needing or asking.

6. Control the process productively

- Arrange the physical surroundings where the discussion of the problem will take place; avoid sitting behind a desk, it becomes a barrier to collaboration and resolution. Stop all interruptions or distractions.
- Set mutually agreed on ground rules: Avoiding personal attacks and accusations; assuming the positive about each other; working toward resolution; no interruptions; describing actions and consequences, not judging....all of which are aimed at moving the process of reconciliation along positively.
- Admit mistakes: *"You are right, I haven't been listening enough to what you have to offer. My being distracted is no excuse for seeming to ignore you. Let's find a way that we can have time together to swap thoughts and discuss your suggestions. I value you and your perspective."*

Criticism is always hard to handle and brings out a very natural fight or flight response. Dealing with criticism in a way that works its way toward resolution of problems is not easy, but its rewards are many and long-lasting.

The Out of Bounds Volunteer
Joan is a volunteer for Court Appointed Special Advocates. She has been working successfully as a volunteer for several years, but the current case to which she has been assigned has touched her heart more deeply than anything she can remember. Theresa, the child whom she is helping through the court system, is the most appealing child Joan has ever met, despite a life of extreme hardship and deprivation. Joan has learned, for example, that Theresa, brought up in extreme poverty, has never had a single Christmas present in her five years of life, and Christmas this year is but three weeks away. In a burst of good spirit, Joan buys Theresa a small doll. presenting it to her during one of their talks. The volunteer manager for CASA finds out about the gift and confronts Joan about the gift, which is clearly in violation of CASA standards prohibiting the purchase of items for clients.

One of the key characteristics of good volunteers is their motivation to work long and hard to achieve goals, particularly in a cause in which they believe. Oddly enough, these same

high levels of motivation can create problem situations.

A frequently occurring example of "good" volunteers who violate organizational policies or rules lies in that volunteer who, in an effort to accomplish the most good for the cause or "their" clients, develops a tendency to go beyond organizational rules or boundaries.

This tendency is most prevalent with volunteers who work closely on a one-to-one basis with clients, because the volunteers are likely to bond more strongly with the clients and their needs than with the agency itself. If the focus of the volunteer is entirely on the needs of the client then they are likely to be very expansive in their definition of what "should" be done to help the client and in their willingness to expand their volunteer role.

While this seems like activity which is done for the best of intentions, it is also activity which is highly dangerous for the agency, the volunteer, and the client. And while correcting such problem behavior risks de-motivating an enthusiastic volunteer, it is essential to do so as quickly as possible.

Here are some suggestions for dealing with this situation:

1. Clearly outline the areas of unacceptable activity. This might include gifts to clients or the performance of volunteer work which is outside the purview of the agency. Very often volunteers will participate in such activity because they don't actually realize that it is wrong. It will very frequently be assistance to a client that looks natural and correct, from the

viewpoint of the helpful volunteer.

2. Indicate to the volunteers the reasons behind the prohibited conduct. Several good ones are maintaining objectivity, avoiding creating unreasonable expectations on the part of clients, and avoiding work for which neither the volunteer or the agency is properly trained.

3. Stress to volunteers that if they find clients with problems outside their core volunteer work they are asked to bring them to the attention of agency staff. Note that while the agency might not be able itself to directly help the clients, it will do its best to find some other method for them receiving support. It is critically important that the volunteer not believe that the agency is "deserting" the clients and their needs.

4. Strictly enforce penalties on those volunteers who are repeat offenders. If you allow these volunteers to get away with conduct outside their job descriptions and outside the policies of the agency you will both encourage further misfeasance on their part and entice other volunteers to break the rules as well. If the volunteer insists on continuing the behavior, let them know that the only way in which they may do so is to separate themselves from the agency, resigning as a volunteer. Do not allow them to tell you that they will only perform the work on their "time off," as this will not necessarily legally separate the agency from the work that is being done.

The Prima Donna
Rick is a valued volunteer at the homeless shelter, mainly because he offers a skill that is unavailable through other means. He is a compute graphics designer, and over the years has created promotional materials for the shelter that have made a significant difference in its public image. But Rick, like many artists, is a perfectionist who is hard to get along with. When upset, he rants and raves, and he *demands to always get his way, particularly when it comes to "his designs." He once held up the printing of a brochure for two months while struggling to find exactly the right photo. As another volunteer once said of him, "He's a legend in his own mind, and to make it worse, he's right."*

We've all encountered the expert who is difficult to deal with, sometimes because their own standards are so high that everyone else fails to meet them, sometimes because they value their own expertise so much that they routinely devalue others.

When a volunteer manager is forced to deal with such a personality, the consequences can be brutal. On one hand, they often bring considerable skills and talents; on the other, they often risk alienating all those around them. Prima donnas can throw temper tantrums, be condescending to others, or make impossible demands. While you may not want to fire them, you often want to strangle them.

Here are some suggestions for working with this difficult volunteer:

1. Recognize that this common type of behavioral problem is often caused by either incredibly high standards or else a deep sense of personal insecurity. Sometimes it is a combination of the two.

2. Consider whether this is a short-term or a long-term problem for you. If the prima donna has been recruited to do a single task and then depart, perhaps living with the situation will be worth the pain. If, on the other hand, the volunteer is entering a possible long-term relationship with you this is a more serious problem, one which will require attempting to change their behavior.

3. If possible, confront the problem behavior as quickly as possible, in a candid but unthreatening way. Tell them that their conduct is detrimental to others and that it is not an acceptable way for interactions within

the organization to take place.

4.   Prima donnas are often quite sensitive, so strive to work through positive reinforcement, rather than any negative actions. Avoid any hint of criticism and use praise as a motivator. The basic insecurity factor will render any criticism both resented and remembered, rather than heeded.

5.   Work to establish good relationships at the start, making sure that you are on the same side and working toward the same vision. Spend more time in the interviewing phase talking about what goals and ideas the prima donna has, to verify that you are indeed thinking in the same direction. Changing the path of a prima donna who is on a roll is a difficult job, indeed.

6.   Try to establish relationships outside the work setting. Sometimes becoming a "friend" is just what the isolated expert needs to establish human contact. Celebrate personal events, such as their birthday or anniversary of starting volunteering. Remember that difficult personalities are often lonely ones.

7.   If the prima donna is alienating those around them, try to isolate their work setting. There are some people who just don't work well with others, but who can produce spectacular results when left to themselves.

When Skill Levels Drop

Mary, an elderly volunteer, has worked at the Historical Society for its entire existence, in fact she is the last one left from the original founding committee. Her specialty all these years has been the Archives, documenting each donation and its history.

Lately, Sue, the volunteer director, has discovered that Mary's records are less and less accurate. Other volunteers are quietly going over her entries each week to correct critical information. These volunteers, who love Mary dearly and appreciate her long dedication, ask Sue to find a way to remove Mary without hurting her feelings.

This problem presents a difficult challenge to Sue and is very typical in many long-standing volunteer programs. Mary is a much beloved volunteer and has been a constant presence through almost 40 years of change and development. She takes great pride in her leadership in the Archives and seems unaware that her ability

to record accurate details has begun to fail.

She would be horrified to realize her actions are causing a problem to Sue and the Society and Sue wants to spare her feelings but knows she need to remove her from her long-held position.

The solution to this dilemma comes from Mary's own love of her village's history and creating records for others to enjoy. In a conversation Sue discovers that Mary's memory surrounding the first years of establishing the Society are as clear as can be. She also finds out that Mary is in contact with the other three surviving members of the founding committee.

Sue then discusses with Mary the fact that she is the last active founding member and it would be remiss of the Society to not capture her memories so that in the future everyone would know all about the efforts, problems and successes she had experienced through the years. She introduces the idea of an oral history.

This thrills Mary who immediately shows just how modern she really is by suggesting that she help create a video record of the memories of all of the other three founders to get different perspectives and then interweave these memories with footage of artifacts first donated to the museum those 40 years ago. (She recalls each item perfectly!)

She also apologizes to Sue about the fact that this project will take so much time she just won't be able to continue on with her Archives job, but has several suggestions for the names of other volunteers she is confident could handle that position.

Sue is relieved and excited about the resolution of the problem and the prospect of an incredible contribution to the museum of the oral--and visual history of the Society.

Mary is thrilled at the prospect of being able to continue to contribute and says a silent "thank you" for a new assignment before anyone notices how poor her eyesight has become, making it more and more difficult to record data accurately.

Often solutions are right in front of people when they are seeking answers to problems. When confronting someone whose skills or abilities are diminishing, the goal becomes four-fold:

- removing them from a position
- still respecting their contributions
- allowing them to retain their dignity
- finding a new placement that permits them to continue to contribute.

Here are some suggestions for dealing with this type of situation:

1. First, try to determine what is really happening. Some indicators may be a clear drop in the abilities of the volunteer, increased absenteeism, reports of difficulty from other volunteers and staff, etc.

2. Second, determine the possible risks if the volunteer is allowed to continue in service. These include risks to clients due to diminished skills and a possible danger to the volunteer from inability to work safely or from personal health problems. Dangers to the volunteer themselves are quite common. Ann Cook, in a study of RSVP volunteer programs, found that 86% of those responding indicated that health concerns of the volunteer were usually the cause of sub-standard performance, forcing the need for retirement or termination.

3. Third, determine if there are other roles that the volunteer can honorably fill, as in the example above. Some roles may involve utilizing the skills and historical experience that the volunteer has acquired (such as in a mentor role), others may involve transferring the volunteer to work that has fewer physical requirements.

4. Fourth, if the decision is made that there is too much risk to the volunteer for them to continue volunteering, then seek support from peers and friends of the volunteer. They may

be able to deal more directly with the situation than you can.

5. And, finally, consider ending the volunteer's relationship with the agency in a ceremonial fashion, honoring the years of service. This is particularly suitable when the volunteer has given a sustained contribution over the years; their service deserves more than dismissal. A ceremony in which they are formally retired, with the name added to the agency "Role of Honor" is more appropriate than termination.

The example above is important for several reasons: First, because it demonstrates that not all solutions to problems require telling the volunteer where they have caused a problem, and secondly because it's a true story. "Mary" had just finished her video history project which involved the local community college video arts department, all three of the other surviving founders and artifacts and records only she could have pulled out of a hat that recorded the history and struggles of the establishment of the Historical Society when she had a stroke. She died shortly afterward, never able to speak again. The park in which the Historical Society's museum stands was named and dedicated in her honor just prior to her stroke. She said it was the proudest day of her life.

The Burnt-Out Case

For the past eight years, Pat has worked one-on-one with some of the most difficult cases that the animal shelter has encountered. She has led the volunteers who accompanied police on raids of puppy mills, and spearheaded efforts to enforce local ordinances against mistreatment of animals. She regards every case where the shelter is unable to find a home for an animal as a personal affront, and often takes animals home to extend their time. She has been totally involved; the shelter has

been her life.

Now, however, Pat is showing signs of wear. She is more and more emotionally distraught when confronted by tough situations. She no longer looks happy about coming to the shelter, but seems to acts more as though it were an unpleasant chore that she must endure. Her conversations with others are short and tense, and often sound more like complaining or whining. She acts like she just doesn't care anymore.

Perhaps the greatest sin in volunteer manager is allowing a good volunteer to self-destruct. The high motivational levels of volunteers are often a potential danger to the volunteer, for they can provoke the volunteer into continuing in service beyond the time when it is healthy to take a break.

Burn-out occurs frequently in volunteer positions which have the following characteristics:

- There is one-on-one work with clients.
- . There is strong emotional bonding with the work, the client, or the cause.
- There is a personal link between the volunteer and the cause, perhaps from a past personal experience.
- The work is relentlessly on-going and never-ending, or under stressful conditions.
- It is difficult to experience any real sense of success from the work.

Marcia Kessler defines burnout as "a withdrawal of energy resulting from the fatigue and frustration brought about by dedication to a job, a cause, a way of life, or even a relationship which ceases to bring the expected rewards."

Very often, the volunteer themselves will not realize that their faculties are beginning to deteriorate. They may be so committed to the work that they cannot contemplate letting the program or the client down. They may be so possessive of the work that they can't bear the thought of not having it to do.

Burnt-out volunteers, in short, are volunteers who have lost their enthusiasm, and while once

good performers are beginning to be more trouble than they are worth. The basic solution to this problem lies in giving the volunteer the time and space to re-charge their depleted energies and enthusiasm.

Here are some ideas for dealing with this situation:

1. Establish set term limits on all volunteer jobs. If a volunteer commitment is for a set limit, this may give the volunteer a sense that they can honorably take a break after they have served their time. It may also give you a formal time at which to talk to the volunteer about taking a break.

2. Establish a policy for vacations for volunteers, and encourage them to take three weeks off during the year. While some will do this naturally, commonly tied to paid employment vacations, others won't think of doing it. You can even establish a policy of allowing longer sabbaticals for volunteers. Tell the volunteer than you'd rather they take a break than become broken. Remind them that the success of the program doesn't depend upon their self-destruction.

3. Practice "re-potting." Like plants, volunteers can't flourish forever in the same soil. Get the volunteer to change jobs, switching from an emotionally-draining one to one which requires different mental or physical skills. Change their environment to one in which they can re-plenish that which has been depleted.

4. Find a new challenge which can re-kindle their interest and sense of excitement. This may involve asking them to step back, reflect on what they have been doing, and offer suggestions of how the program can improve. Ask them to go out and look at similar programs to see what ideas they can gather.

5. Don't be surprised if you encounter resistance from the volunteer when you suggest changes; if a lot of their own ego is invested in what they are doing they will find it difficult to

give up. Be strict in reminding them that any change is ultimately for the good of the program, and that once they are able you want them to return to work, better than ever.

Yadda, Yadda, Yadda

John, a bachelor, was a successful salesman before retiring early and coming to the zoo to volunteer. He asked to be part of the day crew that helped refurbish exhibits and habitats because his hobby had always been building and finishing furniture.

He does a good job but drives everyone crazy with his constant chatter that is distracting. He's now begun to stop by the zoo's volunteer office wanting to chat with the director, Betsi and her secretary plus anyone else who happens to be around.

People are now trying to avoid him and reject all of his invitations to dinner, shows or even coffee. The more he's rejected the more he presses and Betsi can document the loss of some volunteers because of John's incessant chatter.

The problem's getting worse.

It isn't difficult to uncover the real issues in this case:

- John is verbal, lonely and at loose ends. He's desperately needy; he wants relationships.

- Volunteers and staff are trying to avoid John and some are leaving because he is so annoying and aggressive.

- Betsi is losing good volunteers, time and energy because of John's neediness.

When dealing with annoyances such as John presents, there are several steps that can be taken:

1. Look carefully at the placement of volunteers. Just because someone asks to do a particular job is not reason enough to place them there. A careful placement interview should reveal a great deal about a person. In John's case there were a lot of clues - he is single and lives alone, taking early retirement, is very verbal, had a career of selling, persuading and sharing information.

All of this could add up to a placement where his talents could be tapped, possibly in fund raising or hosting or tour guides or liaison with groups and schools wishing to visit the zoo. Working on the exhibits would use his building and design skills but also put him in a very non-verbal, non-social setting.

2. When an obviously needy person is causing a problem their neediness is often both the challenge and the solution. They want to help and be a part of the effort and that can be used by the volunteer manager to re-direct their energies. A plan can often be devised that will allow such a person to have more of their needs met while minimizing their shortcomings and serving the program more effectively.

3. Think through more appropriate placement options. Consider:

- The principle skills needed.
- How their annoying habit (talking) might be used to advantage.
- Who they will work for and with? Look especially at the skills and personality of their supervisor . (In John's case two jobs the director had in mind would cause him to work with a very strong volunteer leader, Elaine, who was very verbal herself, outgoing, organized, charmingly direct, strong and playful.)
- If assignments offer trial involvement opportunities – a way for everyone to try out the match on a small scale.
- What jobs should be eliminated from consideration because they would be damaged by the volunteer's annoying habit?
- What jobs would offer the highest chance for success for the program and the volunteer?

4. Bring the volunteer in for a private, uninter-rupted meeting. Discuss the problem directly and its effects. State the need for a more comfortable placement. Do not allow this point to become a debate - the volunteer cannot keep the current job assignment. Be firm but never cruel; this is a nice person not a nasty one, misguided not evil.

Focus the conversation on the other options for service that can use the skills of the volunteer while meeting the needs of the program (always the volunteer manager's first priority and focus) and the needs of the volunteer.

It is important to distinguish between "mere chattiness" and more serious substantive problems. If, for example, John had a tendency not only to talk but to also breach the confidentiality of the organization or those who worked with it, then the situation is much more significant and would need to be dealt with much more directly.

5. Suggest options that have been well-thought out. In John's case the volunteer manager had settled, with the help of Elaine who would then have direct responsibility for John's work, on two options:

• Liaison for groups to encourage them to tour the zoo. This job would allow John to talk to many people, interact socially, use his skills in sales to persuade them to visit and work rather independently calling on groups.

• Being a tour guide at the zoo for groups visiting. This job would also meet his need to be social, allow him to talk to many people and work rather independently from other volunteers.

Betsi had ruled out the following positions:

✗ Fundraising - the goal at the zoo was to make friends with the community, and this included their fund raising plans. Even if a potential donor said "no" to an appeal, it was the goal of the development department to make sure they felt like friends of the zoo. Betsi was concerned John would press so hard to get funds that they would never feel very friendly toward the institution!

✗ Hosting-those people who simply stand at key intersections in the zoo and answer questions, direct people etc. Again Betsi felt this was not the best placement as many people only want their questions answered quickly and not have to deal with the excessive chatter she felt John would force on them.

6. If there is more than one option available, suggest a trial period in which the volunteer could do each job a few times and then meet with their supervisor and the volunteer manager to make a permanent position decision. (Permanent for now. Jobs need to have a time limit of one year to allow re-evaluation, a new placement or re-assignment.)

In John's case, both positions required extensive training on all aspects of the zoo which, because the trainings were led by Elaine who would be John's supervisor, afforded everyone some time to readjust and for Elaine to view John's behavior directly. In the end (yes this is a true story) John became the zoo's best recruiter of groups, exciting them about coming to visit and even making sure he was on hand to greet them when they arrived. After two years in the position he asked to specialize in approaching schools because he discovered a wonderful rapport with young children. He added the component of a pre-visit talk in the classroom where he excited the children and educated them in what to watch for during their upcoming visit to his beloved zoo.

In John's third year in this position he was named volunteer of the year at the zoo.

In his 5th year, the city honored him as one of their citizens of the year. He is, to this day, called "Mr. Zoo."

Not all stories will have as spectacular an ending, but it does emphasize that some of the most annoying problems can be turned around by careful examination, a distinction between the problem and the person (not a wrong person, a right person in a wrong job), a determination to meet program needs first but with room to also meet the volunteer's need, laying out options and trying them out for success.

This story also illustrates the importance of the social factor in volunteer motivation.

Volunteers tend to be people who enjoy being with other people, and view volunteering as part of their social life. Interacting with others is a natural result of this inclination, and for some volunteers may be their major reason for volunteering.

Those who supervise volunteers need to realize that part of their obligation to the volunteer will lie in assisting in providing a social network for the volunteer. A good volunteer manager will consider the following:

- Identifying those volunteers with high social needs during the interviewing process. These volunteers should be assigned to positions that allow interaction with others. A simple way to do this is to ask potential volunteers whether they prefer working alone or with others.

- Scheduling time for visiting and relating with volunteers. This "mothering" function is well-known to experienced volunteer managers, and can be essential in building long-term relationships with volunteers. It is essential to remind those who will be managing volunteers to block time out of their own schedules when they will be available to the volunteers.

- Developing events and activities that allow volunteers to interact with each other. One good example of this is having a designated "volunteer room" where volunteers can gather and talk about what they are doing. Another method is to organize volunteer "reflection" groups based around common positions or clients, in which volunteers meet periodically to discuss what they have been doing.

Providing these outlets for the volunteers' social needs will both help control some problem volunteer behavior and strengthen overall bonding of volunteers with each other and with the agency.

The Resentful Former Peer

Andy started volunteering at the Food Bank when it was first started, three years ago. At the time he was in college and it was his first volunteer effort. As he continued to volunteer, he gradually discovered that he had a talent for organizing others and started helping coordinate the various volunteer teams who came in. Three months ago, the volunteer manager at the Food Bank announced she was leaving, and offered Andy, who was just graduating from college, the opportunity to take over her position. Andy accepted the challenge.

During his first weeks, however, Andy discovered that one of the volunteers with whom he used to work with on a friendly basis was beginning to act quite oddly toward him.

The volunteer seemed to avoid Andy, and looked resentful when Andy talked with him about work assignments. Andy has also heard that the volunteer is disparaging him behind his back to other volunteers.

Going from being "one of the gang" to being "the boss" is one of the most difficult transitions in management. This transition can occur when:

- You're promoted to a higher level in your program or agency, one which places you in a supervisory role over others, particularly when you used to be a co-worker to these people.

- You're a volunteer who has been asked to "manage" other volunteers or even to coordinate the entire volunteer program. Many of your neighbors also volunteer for the agency.

- You're a member of a group who has been elected to a leadership position, such as an officer or a committee chair. You've recruited some of your best friends to serve on the committee with you.

In each case, the nature of the relationship between you and other people has just changed, and changed dramatically. The Latin phrase for this is *primus inter pares*, "first among equals," implying the new difference in status and power that has emerged. In some ways, the greater the degree of friendship you had with your former colleagues the more difficult the transition will be.

Difficulties will occur both for you, the promoted person, and for your former peers. Each will have to adopt to a new way of relating to one another which takes into account the new reality - one person now has some authority and responsibility over the others and over coordinating the work that the group will seek to accomplish. You have become that most feared of individuals: "The Boss."

Here are some tips for making this transition go more smoothly and successfully:

1. Begin cultivating support before you're selected for the position. Make your intentions known, and discuss your plan with your friends. Trying to advance in the world is nothing to be ashamed of, nor is having talents for administration than can be of value to the organization. One of the worst things that can happen is to "surprise" your friends with a sudden rise in position. You'll catch them off-guard and make it look as if you were abandoning them without notice. If you yourself don't know until the last moment about the promotion (because you aren't asked to apply but are simply offered the position), ask for time to consider the offer and use that time to talk with friends and colleagues.

2. If there is a selection process for the position, try to find out everything you can about it, both before applying and after you have been selected. Your position will be easier if the selection process has been "fair" - if everyone was encouraged to apply, if there was equal weight given to all applications, if a real effort was made to find the most-qualified candidate, etc. When you have been selected, ask why you were chosen. You may be able to use this information to explain to others why you and not they were picked. You should also try to find out who else in your department or group might have applied for the position.

3. Recognize for yourself that you are about to face a change in position, with a different kind of responsibility. You are not abandoning your friends and colleagues, but you will be relating to them in a somewhat different fashion. You are now responsible to the organization for managing the efforts of this, and this may occasionally not mesh perfectly with your obligations or relationships with your friends. You will need to consciously make a decision about how much "space" or "distance" you will keep from your former colleagues. Talk to other supervisors who you respect about what works for them. You will also need to find out the "style" at your organization - does everyone operate informally as equals or is there in fact a hierarchy? You may not choose to operate yourself according to the "culture" of the agency, but you should know enough to determine what it is before you develop your own style of relating to others.

4. The most important time period for new managers is the first week in their new position. Even if you already know the people involved, you will still be making a "first impression" on them at this point. How you act toward them and how you structure your interactions will mold the relationship that develops. Their uncertainly will

be very high at this point, so you will particularly need to clarify roles and expectations, both as a group and in individual meetings. Call a meeting of your new "staff" as soon as possible after your promotion - on the first day if possible.

At the meeting, let people know your own feelings about your promotion, outline your ideas about the goals and objectives the group will be working on, and present your expectations

regarding any changes that you anticipate. If you will be operating with a clearly different style from your predecessor, let people know your preferences. Be careful about announcing too many changes at this first meeting - it will be better to give yourself time to talk individually to your group and solicit their opinions as well about what needs to be changed.

If you suspect there are hard feelings, invite discussion of the subject. Look for non-verbal signals that some people are not happy with the situation and privately invite these people to share their feelings and concerns with you at a later time. Do not, however, apologize for being placed in charge. You'll need to believe that you're the right person for the job in order to make others believe it as well. This does not mean attempting to look infallible or all-knowing - there may be people who are much more knowledgeable about some areas than you in the group, but your skill will lie in helping these people make the best use of their knowledge and talents.

5.   Arrange individual meetings with each person in your unit to talk about their work. Ask for their input regarding what needs to be

done and how you can be of help to them in their work. Ask them how they see themselves best making a contribution to the group. Note that you will be relying on them for their expertise and their support. Let them know how you like to be communicated with and ask them how you can best communicate with them. If they have had a special position or responsibility, talk with them about how they will be continuing with this role. Remember that many of these people will have experienced a comfortable working relationship with your predecessor that has now disappeared, so you may expect some fear and uncertainty on their part.

6.   If you do encounter someone who remains resistant to you, confront them privately and directly. Let them express their feelings, but then let them know that the time for discussion is past and the time to work together has arrived. Ask them how they see things working out successfully and what they are willing to do to make the new relationship work. Note that any continuation of complaint or reluctance on their part damages the work effort of all and will not be allowed to continue. One way to give them an option is to ask whether they would like your help in being "transferred" to some other unit or your suggestions for another agency in which to volunteer.

7.   Adjust your behavior to match your new position. Make sure that you are equally fair to all, and especially to those with whom you were in competition. Being "fair" means neither treating them too harshly nor too well. If you have been closer to some colleagues than to others, you will need to make sure you pay equal attention to those who weren't your friends. As a supervisor you have an equal responsibility to all and cannot appear to play favorites. This appearance of fairness can be reflected in little behaviors - who, for example, do you have lunch with? Who do you give the "best" assignments to? Who spends more time in your office?

8.   Involving others in discussing and making decisions is a good supervisory technique. Be aware, however, that in your early days, others will be watching to see how you involve the group in making decisions. They will attempt to determine whether you want and listen to input, whether you value ideas that may run counter to your own, how you deal with opposition and whether you are willing to face and make tough decisions.

You must find a way to involve others, but you must also show your own willingness to take a stand and even to make an unpopular decision that needs to be made. Too accommodating a decision-making style can be as ineffective and as unpopular as a too dictatorial one. One of the reasons that groups have leaders is to have a person willing and able to make difficult decisions when the group is unwilling or unable to reach consensus. You can't be a leader if you won't lead.

While renegotiating your relationships with your previous peers, you should also remember that you are entering into a new set of relationships with others as well. You must also be developing a relationship with your new "peer" group, the other leaders in your organization. These are your new co-workers, with whom you must coordinate the work that you are doing and with whom you must jointly plan the management activities. Many of the steps suggested above can be adopted and applied to cultivating a working relationship with other managers.

Three Steps to Correcting Actions of Problem Volunteers

There are many ways to intervene in working to redirect the energies of problem volunteers. As first discussed in *New Competencies for Volunteer Administrators* here is a simple three-step approach:

1. Talk with the volunteer in private. Document the effects of their actions. Remind them of their commitment to the cause and the people it serves as well as the need for the program to function at the highest level of effectiveness.

Give them time to respond, telling why they chose the actions they did. Inquire about any circumstances that may not have been apparent to anyone but them. Avoid accusatory statements. Never "attack" them. Keep the focus on the actions and consequences. Take notes openly and move toward setting next steps for corrective action. Agree on a next meeting

within a month to track their progress. Make sure your language assumes the positive resolution of the problem. Establish ways to measure new behavior and explain that not changing their actions will result in dismissal. End on a statement of confidence in their ability to become an even more valuable contributor to the program's goals. A process of this sort is especially effective in dealing with such minor, but annoying, performance problems as the volunteer who is constantly coming in late.

If in this first meeting, it becomes apparent that the volunteer simply wants "out" find a graceful way to allow them to move on to some other assignment or take a "sabbatical" from the program. If belligerence is their response, suggest they move on to some other community effort immediately. Keep control of the situation.

2. At a second meeting with those volunteers who say they are willing to work on correcting their actions, review goals agreed to in meeting one and document progress. If none has been made ask why and what would help them move toward the adjustments needed. Re-contract for specific changes in behavior by putting the new agreement in writing. Document specific problems and results and the consequence of dismissal. Copy the letter to a supervisor. Agree to meet in a very short time - possibly 10 days.

3. At the third meeting applaud any success toward the agreed on goals. If some of the goal has not been met, ask the reason why, state this as unacceptable and tell them they will be monitored for a week to insure all of the behavioral changes required are in place.

If none of the goals have been reached, remind them of the previously stated consequence of removal from their position. Thank them for their previous service if this is appropriate, write up your actions and allow them to leave. If there is a concern about retribution have them sign a copy of the letter they received after the second meeting in which problems, required actions and consequences were spelled out. (Progress notes would have been added in this

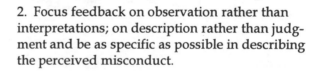

third meeting that document the non-compliance.) If they refuse to sign it to acknowledge their understanding of the issues raised, call in a witness to attest to this refusal.

Giving and Receiving Feedback

In dealing with problems involving volunteers, there must be dialogue among those affected. To lead these dialogues productively, the volunteer manager must have the ability to move conflicts toward resolution. A critical skill to facilitate this is the ability to give and receive feedback, the reflective data one gets or gives related to behavior. As Kathy Brown notes, "Almost everyone who takes on a job wants to do it well, and volunteers will stay longer, feel more satisfied, and be of greater help to the organization if they receive constructive feedback from those who supervise them."

Feedback can provide learning opportunities as we look into the mirror that it affords us...."to see ourselves as others see us." Frequently we do not have the benefit of this reflection and thus never understand that *How* we say or do things is as important as *What* we say and do.

If a volunteer manager is trying to win support for a merger between the hospital volunteer program and the auxiliary how they or others involved present their idea is as important as what they present.

A key volunteer attends the board meeting and presents the idea of merger:

"The auxiliary may have been important years ago but it's irrelevant and out of step with the times. It needs to simply give it up and disband. We can absorb any left over auxilians into our volunteer program here at the hospital."

Obviously, the volunteer manager is horrified as she had presented the idea to individuals in this more positive light: *"The volunteers who work through the hospital volunteer program and those who work as auxilians share the same goal of service to the hospital and its patients. It seems to me that by merging our strengths and efforts we can all be more effective in our service and benefit from each others strong points: the longer perspectives and community contacts of the auxilians and the younger energies and networking of the volunteer corps."*

If no one offers feedback on the two approaches

offered above, the volunteer may never understand the negative impact the first example offers nor will the volunteer manager understand fully how positively her approach has been received.

The following are suggestions for good feedback:

1. Focus feedback on behavior rather than the person.

"Your presentation on the merger had a very negative impact, especially when it included the accusation of irrelevance of the auxiliary."

not...

"I can't believe you were so thoughtless in telling the auxiliary they were irrelevant. Are you cruel or just stupid?"

The key rule in giving feedback that will be heeded is to criticize the work, not the worker. This means you must not appear to be attacking or threatening the worker, rather you must focus on discussing how to improve the quality of the work itself.

2. Focus feedback on observation rather than interpretations; on description rather than judgment and be as specific as possible in describing the perceived misconduct.

"I myself felt angry when the auxiliary was branded 'irrelevant' and saw others in the room respond the same."

not....

"It's obvious that you're threatened by the auxiliary and want it out of your hair. I'll bet you've never even looked into their history or what they've done to help our hospital."

3. Focus feedback on as timely s basis as possible. Tie feedback to a specific time and place and do it as close to the occurrence as possible.

"I want us to talk about your comments on the merger that you offered at yesterday's board meeting ."

not...

"You have been making bad presentations all year and never seem to learn from them."

4. Focus feedback on the sharing of information rather than giving advice. By sharing information (observations, behaviors, consequences, impacts, etc.) the other person is allowed the opportunity to draw conclusions on their own rather than being told what to do. Telling someone what to do suggests they are not smart enough to figure it out for themselves.

If they really don't know what to do they will probably signal this quandary, allowing the volunteer manager to ask them if they would like some suggestions.

5. Focus feedback on looking at alternatives rather than quick answers or solutions. Help people form a list of options and alternatives to problem behavior; the heat of conflict and possible defensiveness may not be the best time to settle on a solution that may prove to be too restrictive and narrow in the future. Set a time to discuss the best option, possibly after several have been tried.

6. Focus the feedback on benefits to the recipient rather than the release it gives the feedback provider. This is not about "getting it off my chest" or "Well, I've done my part in setting her straight. What happens next is out of my hands." It's about the needs of the recipient, not the feedback provider. Stress the need for quality service to the clients.

7. Focus the amount of feedback on what the recipient can handle and absorb. Don't overwhelm a volunteer or staff member with too much information at once. The goal is not to tell them everything that can be shared, but to give them an amount of information that they can absorb, process and use effectively.

8. Watch the timing of feedback: Giving good feedback at the wrong time can cause more harm than good. Trying to tell someone they need to improve their telephone skills the day after they come back from a parent's funeral is a sure way to lose their support and anyone else's who hears about this. Setting up unreasonable deadlines for changing performance is also non-productive - it guarantees failure and resentment. Develop planned deadlines for change, and then follow-through on these deadlines to see what performance has altered.

9. Avoid making a recipient wonder why they are getting feedback: If the feedback giver is vague, has a hidden agenda or is trying to talk around the real issue, the receiver will sense this and not hear the feedback itself because they are wondering what this is really all about. Be honest and direct in feedback and avoid sub-texts, hints and inferences.

10. Focus the feedback on positives, rather than negatives. Don't just criticize the volunteer for what they have done wrong in the past, since changing the past is beyond anyone's capability. Instead focus on what might be done better in the future. Describe challenges as growth opportunities or ways to make the volunteer's contribution even greater. Use "praise sandwiches" in which you alternate positive comments about the volunteer's performance with discussions of what is not meeting expectations.

11. Focus on maintaining good relationships while stressing the need for quality performance. Imagine that someone were directing this feedback to you and ask yourself how you would prefer it to be worded and explained. Listen to the viewpoint of the volunteer and offer sympathy for their problems and difficulties.

12. Focus on the consequences of the volunteer not correcting their behavior. While the intent is to be as amicable as possible during this session, it is also important to stress upon the volunteer the seriousness of the situation. They should not leave thinking that they are off the hook. Note that this discussion is the beginning

of the corrective process, not the conclusion. Indicate that more serious steps will be implemented if the volunteer does not make acceptable progress by the agreed-upon deadlines.

Giving and receiving feedback is a critical skill needed for effective, focused volunteer management. It makes communication and relation-

cused on
reduces
s workers
r."

ictive to
e dealing
style that
is not a true
ult or delib-
ase, the
ning to live
fficulties to

iculty
, and is not.
two dispa-
ecific incid-

agreement
ese to build
a bridge, or at least affect an accommodation.

3. Keep conversations based on issues, not personalities. Avoid areas of controversy, if possible. Don't get involved in irrelevant arguments.

4. Keep things simple and clear to avoid any misunderstanding. Put things in writing and read over them to make sure they are easily understood.

5. Keep your own attitude positive and rehearse positive interactions before the meeting. Make sure both body and verbal language are in agreement. Don't let old attitudes interfere with your current effort.

6. Speak in private if a difficult issue must be resolved.

7. Don't take their dislike personally.

8. Remember that you are not God. "Winning" may only mean arranging a tolerable working relationship, not solving all their personality defects.

Keys to Motivation

Dealing with those who are annoying may also involve finding ways to motivate them toward better performance. The best ways to accomplish this are:

1. *Ask for performance.* Indicate that both you and the organization have quality standards and that you expect everyone to meet or exceed them.

2. *Use lots of positive reinforcement - and personalize it.* Congratulate the volunteer when they do perform well, and express surprise and disappointment when they fail to perform adequately. Note that others in the program are relying on them.

3. *Build relationships.* Get to know the volunteer so you can talk to them as a friend. Indicate that you personally are disappointed in their performance, but will be willing to work with them to achieve improvement.

4. *Understand the volunteer's point of view.* Remember that this is a two-way street. Ask the volunteer what you can do to make their work better, and be prepared for them to suggest some changes that may be unexpected to you.

5. *Model what you want* Don't preach what

you don't practice, and don't require of one volunteer what you are also not requiring of others.

6.   *Refuse to accept poor performance*. Draw a line in the sand and defend it. Volunteers will only know you are serious if you set limits and enforce them.

Conclusion
These first types of volunteer are essentially those who have the normal human range of quirks, but who can provide a valuable asset to the organization if their skills and personalities can be meshed with others. Good management is the art of finding and re-directing the talents and interests of these people, and blending them into the harmonious fabric of the agency.

Chapter Four
The Seriously Disruptive Volunteer

Introduction
This chapter deals with problem volunteers who pose a more significant challenge and threat to the organization. It discusses problem volunteers who can create serious difficulties in both the short and long term, and then discusses techniques such as conflict resolution and evaluation of volunteers that may prove helpful in handling these types of problem situations.

Founder's Syndrome
Peggy is hired to head an arts center. Her biggest champion, coach & mentor is an elderly woman on the board that everyone seems to honor. Sweet, nurturing and supportive, the woman seems to love everything Peggy does.

At the board's annual meeting Peggy suggests that the Christmas Bach festival, in its 23rd year but attracting diminishing support from the community, be changed to a broader scope of music and diversity. Peggy's champion pales and speaks against the change at the meeting. After that she escalates her objections, calling on long-time supporters to ask their help in defeating the change. She also begins to suggest that Peggy was not "right" for her job, hinting but not actually being specific about "things I know that I just don't want to share about poor Peggy." Everything Peggy tries to do in any area, her past mentor sabotages; even though she remains sweet to her face, it's stab, stab, stab in the back.

What Peggy had run into was the Founder Syndrome. Had she done her homework before suggesting a change to the Bach Festival she would have discovered that the sweet elderly lady-turned-Attila-the-Hun had founded that festival in the face of great resistance in the community. In her mind her prominence was wedded to the festival; it was, in her eyes, her "claim to fame."

To understand the Founder Syndrome there has to be an understanding of what Dr. Inamura of Japan labels his *Theory of Significance.* The good Doctor, one of the world's experts on suicide, tells us that when people feel their significance has been taken from them they often believe their life is over. Because of such confusion between their worth and their work, they will fight ferociously when anyone "threatens" whatever they see as their significance. Peggy found that out the hard way!

When someone has an over-reaction to something there can be many reasons for it, but the Founder Syndrome may be most likely. A person who was instrumental in bringing something about (a program, an award, an event, a major shift in the organization or (Heaven's forbid) the founding of the organization itself!) has an ownership that runs very deeply and often is seen as something that needs to be protected like a child.

Whenever a volunteer manager is about to suggest changes, they must go into the group's archives or someone's memory to find out what history the existing effort has had. For change to occur and something new to be introduced, something old often has to go. Before such a change is even hinted, find out who was involved in the creation of the old effort.

If a volunteer director, in researching the group's history, does indeed find that one or more of the current volunteers or paid staff was instrumental in establishing that which is to be changed, they are wise to tread carefully. Here are some suggestions:

1. Assess the current influence of the founders.

Handling Problem Volunteers

Who do they impact the most? Who influences them? What clout do they have?

2. Are they still wedded to the old idea? When a conversation comes up surrounding their original idea, what is their reaction? If it has not been discussed in your presence, bring it up casually and watch for their reaction. It's possible they have thought for a long time it should be dropped or changed, and thus can be the strongest possible ally in suggesting modification.

3. If the reaction of this founder is defensiveness or, worse yet, the "wounded warrior" response, be alerted to a long road ahead for any change. Begin to identify those key people needed to effect change, including anyone who might be able to influence the founder. The founder may never offer outright support, but at least any sabotage might be deflected.

4. Since the real issue in the example is significance, what other ways might be devised to bring recognition to the founder? Could Peggy have suggested the holiday concert be re-named in honor of the original founder of the event? Could change be gradually introduced in this newly named event, featuring Bach but also introducing newer music that would trace the development of the arts center through the years? What sincere honor that is highly and permanently visible in the community could be given to such a prominent contributor?

It would also be wise for Peggy to have a contingency plan if nothing seems to work to reduce the founder's resistance. It is always possible that good ideas will simply have to wait until a more likely timing for success.

5. If a founder is still in charge of the effort they began years ago, volunteer directors may have an even tougher time introducing any change. The issue then becomes a double whammy: Significance and Control. The founder not only sees the effort as their claim to fame, they still have total control of how it is managed. As time goes on, and their influence or popularity declines, they may become more and more desperate about hanging on to the effort others believe needs to be changed or dropped.

Tread carefully with this challenge, since it is fraught with land mines! Present the case for change in a light of honoring the effort's incredible contributions through the years and the reasons which can be documented of dropping it. Instead of focusing on its demise, focus on a long period of transition that honors the founder publicly; then hold one last occurrence and a celebration of the event's history and contribution. Make the founder the center of attention, invite those who wish to honor his/her vision and leadership and spotlight what continuing efforts were made possible by the effort's existence.

Often we move too quickly in setting aside an effort, without giving any sensitivity to the people who gave blood, sweat and tears to bring that effort to life and lead it through the years. If it also was something that they continually had control over and offered them notoriety, it is much like wrenching a child from their arms.

Find creative, sensitive and caring ways to express gratitude for all founders have done, allow them to control their effort for a period of time, then plan a celebration that honors their contributions publicly. The event will be bitter sweet for them, but at least there will not be bloodshed for those who suggested the change.

The Gender/Race Problem

George is a senior volunteer who has come to the senior home as a volunteer after years of helping coach soccer and Little League baseball. He is still a boisterous, outgoing man, with a tendency to get close to people and talk directly with them. He also has a tendency to touch people as he talks with them. One of the younger female volunteers at the home is disturbed by this, believing that George's actions in dealing with her go beyond good taste. She doesn't like the comments George makes about her appearance, or the jokes that he tells or the way he gets close to her and puts his hands on her shoulder sometimes as he talks to her. She complains to the volunteer manager about how she is feeling.

Unwelcome sexual advances have made their way into the volunteer work environment, just as they have in paid situations. And, as in paid situations, they are often one of the most difficult areas for a manager to deal with.

Sexual harassment is usually defined as any unwelcome sexual advances, requests for sexual or other favors, or other verbal or physical conduct of a sexual nature. Sexual harassment includes verbal harassment (epithets, derogatory comments, slurs, demeaning jokes), physical harassment (assaults, impeding movement, or any physical interference with normal work movement) and visual harassment (derogatory posters, cartoons, drawings, etc.).

While in the situation outlined above it is entirely possible that George has no intention of sexual harassment, his behavior certainly has resulted in the perception of harassment by the female volunteer, and needs to be dealt with. Commonly included as actions which constitute sexual harassment are:

- joking or making sexually related comments at or around others
- staring or leering at anyone
- dating other workers, especially subordinates
- talking to others about the details of their relationships or sex lives
- touching other employees
- engaging in sexually-oriented banter

Dealing with this situation is a two-sided effort.

The first requirement is a set of clearly outlined policies and expectations around sexual interactions. These policies should be the same for both volunteers and staff and should be covered as part of the orientation for all volunteers. The best resource for examining such policies is Linda Graff's *By Definition: Policies for Volunteer Programs*, but they are also readily available from any personnel department.

The second requirement is being willing to talk with volunteers about their conduct. In our example, as is often the case, the chances are very good that George is totally unaware of the reactions to his conduct. He comes from a dif-

ferent environment, one in which such comments are part of normal conversation, and his attempts to be complimentary are probably well meant. As a former sports volunteer, he is accustomed to physical conduct as a method of building camaraderie.

Clearly a conversation with George is in order. This is the type of situation which we include among the seriously disruptive because many volunteer managers, realizing that George does not intend to harass, will be unwilling to confront the issue. At this point the situation graduates from the annoying to the more dangerous and disruptive.

The volunteer manager needs to have a private conversation with George in which the results of his actions are pointed out to him, followed by a request that George be more considerate of the feelings of others. The really smart volunteer manager won't wait for a complaint to have this conversation, but will proactively engage George in a discussion as soon as conduct that might offend others is exhibited.

Intentional Prejudice or Harassment
Our example with George is a rather gentle one, which unfortunately can manifest itself in much more disruptive ways. Take, for example, the problem of bigotry.

The Thorndike-Barnhart Dictionary defines being bigoted as "sticking to an opinion, belief, etc., with reason and not tolerating other views; intolerant; prejudiced."

When looking at the issue of bigotry, bigots or being bigoted as it relates to volunteer programs, the topic must be as clear as possible, unclouded by anything that even hints at an excuse for such behavior. It must be simple and to the point.

Rather than provide an example, the reader is asked to simply let their mind go back to their encounters with bigots through the years. Everyone has had such run-ins and though their faces and the objects of their bigotry would differ, such people have commonalities that are easily recognizable:

• Some other person, group or identifiable segment of society is "bad" or "evil" in their opinion.

• These "others" are blamed for every societal ill, or problem the bigot has ever had or the reason the bigot cannot do a good or complete or acceptable job. It is always the "others" fault.

• Rarely is the bigot's prejudice limited to one person or group; they spread their intolerance around to multiple sources, allowing them to rant and rave in many categories.

• They will not listen to reason; they don't believe in facts.

• They generalize. If cut off in traffic by a driver in a white Honda, they then have a new target for their hatred - all drivers of white Honda's who, by the end of the day have been blamed for all wars, disease, pestilence, poverty and sour milk since 1906.

• They find many convoluted ways to bring

their prejudice into any and all discussions; a conversation about what theme to have for the volunteer recognition banquet somehow has the bigot dropping in disparaging words about the target group of the day. It dumbfounds most listeners.

• They can never understand why people avoid them or why they have trouble with relationships. Typically, they eventually conclude it is somehow the fault of those "others" who have made their life so miserable.

• They are blamers. Nothing is ever their fault; they avoid consequences that they have earned by their behavior by placing blame for any problems on those dastardly "others" who are plotting against them in their mind.

Readers can add to the list from their own experience. Whatever their shape or makeup, bigots are part of the global world in which our volunteer programs exist and therefore, can find their way into such programs either as volunteers, paid staff, donors, board members, supporters, suppliers, etc. There is no insurance to prevent bigots from appearing at our door.

The question becomes: What can be done about such bigots? The answer is easier to state than to accomplish.

Get rid of them:

1. Check out any reports of bigoted statements or actions that come from an individual. Verify them. Investigate to discover if previous occurrences in this vein have been reported. Is there a pattern of behavior emerging?

2. Confirm through other eye witnesses that the reported behavior did indeed occur.

3. Document the occurrence. Give specific details of the action with the corroboration of as many witnesses as possible.

4. Confront the accused offender with the evidence. Respond in one of two ways with what they say in return:

• If their response confirms their bigotry by further statements reaffirming the reported prejudice ("Of course I said that; those [others] are lazy bums and everyone knows it! I won't deny I said what was reported...that's the facts!") then begin termination procedures. First, reassign them to a job that removes them from contact with volunteers or others who would be contaminated by such bigotry. Monitor their behavior closely. Document any further grievances; make sure any meeting with them has a witness that can attest to the fairness and clarity of the message of unacceptability and consequences. It may be wise to audio tape conversations for the not-unheard-of possibility of the bigot attempting to shift blame to the supervisor at a later date.

- If the response of the accused is that they were misunderstood or they deny saying what has been reported, ask for their version of the occurrence. Present the evidence on file and ask them to explain why they feel the accusers would have reported such things. Consider bringing the accusers and accused together to try to get to the truth. If it comes down to one's word against another's, explain verbally and later in writing that future activities will be monitored, and should any prejudicial actions be witnessed in the future, dismissal will result. Also make it clear to the accuser, that any sense that accusations have been manufactured will also be dealt with severely. This latter step would only come when the volunteer program manager felt there was some reason to doubt the veracity of the accuser. Proceed to monitor as promised, asking for feedback from multiple colleagues in a position to experience either person.

When confronting bigots, avoid:

1. Trying to talk them out of their bigotry. It wastes time and probably annoys them. It will certainly annoy you.

2. Trying to debate their prejudice. Debating

suggests some credence to opposing views. There is never any credence to the unfairness of bigotry.

3. Allowing them to bring in other issues. Stay focused on the specific actions in question.

4. Lengthy or ambiguous conversation. Stick to the incident, speak clearly and plainly, avoid anything less than direct communication.

When Bigotry is Subtle
On occasion, a volunteer manager will encounter someone who is rather clever at hiding their prejudice. When confronted, they will deny bigotry, believing that they have been sneaky enough to give themselves "cover" that masks their intolerance.

It will take more effort in such cases to document and find specific examples of their bigotry, but if they are truly prejudiced, their actions and language will eventually trip them up. Watch for patterns of avoiding any single category of "others" such as people from the opposite sex, ethnic, religious, cultural, economic or political category.

Bigotry is a cancer that can eat away at any group. It so offends others that it not only makes overt enemies for the bigot but also causes people to avoid programs in which such bigots are tolerated. There can be a silent exodus of volunteers, supporters or staff who conclude that staying involved is a greater price than they are willing to pay.

When the Bigot Beast appears in any program, the only solution is to turn it out as quickly as possible!

The Liar
Jane has been assigned the job of clearing a community event by contacting key groups, the Chamber of Commerce, the School Board, etc. as well as key individuals to make sure there are no conflicts with the dates considered for the event. She reports that there is no problem, and in fact, those contacted are enthusiastic about the plans.

As time goes by however, John, the volunteer direc-

tor, begins to take calls from people who have just heard about the event and are unhappy because it comes on top of some of their own plans. John is shocked to find that they were never actually contacted by Jane.

John asks Jane about it and she insists she talked with them. The event draws near and real resistance grows to supporting it, again based on the fact that key groups were never informed about it. John sits down with Jane and presents this information. Jane again insists she spoke with these groups and acts bewildered at John's concern. She looks him in the eyes and though vague about the exact dates of contact, insists she spoke with them.

Jane is lying.

The Difficulty of Dealing With People Who Lie

One of the most frustrating challenges before volunteer directors is to have to deal with someone who is lying. First of all, it is typically outside the director's way of thinking; they tend to believe what people say and trust them to tell the truth.

Secondly, it can be very hard to prove. Reconstructing events about who did what when is time and energy consuming as well as distasteful.

Fortunately lying rarely happens. Unfortunately, it will almost certainly happen at least once during a volunteer director's tenure.

Alarmists, pessimists, and the legal department of most organizations would have managers at any level constantly be suspicious, assuming the need to plan for liars at every turn. That simply is not part of the nature of most volunteer directors as it would require documenting every tiny action, having a "witness" to all conversations with every worker, paid or volunteer and bugging the lapel flower of every manager to "catch" people being bad!.

Instead, less stringent precautions can be taken

that can protect a volunteer manager against liars, though nothing can totally guarantee that they never have to deal with them. Here are some suggestions:

1. *Put all assignments in writing.* The best insurance that things will be done in a timely and honest fashion comes in the form of a simply-stated, explicit job design that is time-lined and available for everyone involved to see. A master timeline can be invaluable as it lists each person, their contact number, job assignments and when jobs are to be done week by week. This shows who does what and when and demonstrates the interdependence of worker assignments. It becomes a recognition tool as people see all that is being done by others; a management tool for key leaders who have an overview of their work as spread out among several volunteers; makes it easier to evaluate steps toward completion; and most importantly, holds people accountable to the world.

2. *Continually check on progress.* Build in checkpoints along the way to insure what has been reported as "done" really has been accomplished. Keep in mind that a better word for communication is interpretation, so the volunteer assigned a job may have done what they believe to be the assignment, but have missed the mark in what was intended to be done by planners. In the example above, it could be that by writing a letter to key groups, Jane thought she indeed had "contacted" them, where John intended that personal conversations be held to insure communication.

3. *Keep notes on results of checkpoints so that there is a written record to refer to for anything questioned in the future.* If at any time there is an example of not telling the entire truth about an effort or there is a sense that the volunteer is giving feedback that seems improbable or defensive, check it out. Ask for direct confirmation without becoming accusatory. If there is resistance or specific non-compliance, take more direct steps to check on the veracity of what was reported.

4. *Set deadlines for specific steps to be taken that could confirm or reject claims that work has been done.* When meetings are held, invite another person to be present to insure that what is being said is clear, direct and understood. Document actions taken to correct any missteps caused by work not really being completed. Openly take notes on any agreements for further action. Follow-up these verbal agreements in writing and copy them to at least one key leader in the organization's hierarchy.

5. *If a pattern of blaming circumstances or others arises, know that this volunteer will probably have to be removed from the assignment.* If that is the case, the documentation done during previous meetings and the clear job assignment at the start will back up the decision for removal. It is very rare, but not unheard of for a volunteer to bring a suit against a volunteer director and organization for being fired. Handle the firing of a volunteer as carefully as the firing of a paid worker, and with as much fairness, understanding and caution.

6. *If a person who has lied admits the falsehoods and does not blame anyone but themselves, they may be able to be salvaged by placing them in another role within the program.* Often someone has gotten "in over their head" in a job assignment, and because they are embarrassed and want to help in any way, they cannot admit that they are being asked to do something beyond their capabilities.

7. *Avoid personal attacks when addressing the person.* Focus on the work assignments and discuss the effects of not getting them done. Personal attacks will only bring out defensiveness; remember, the volunteer is not a "bad" person, but more likely a good person in a bad assignment match. For people to be successful their skills, likes and capabilities need to match the demands of the work assigned.

8. *Try to figure out specifically why the volunteer found it necessary to lie about progress in their assignment.* Could it be that the job design was unclear? Could it be that the expectations of everyone are unrealistic? Is it possible that the hierarchy is making assumptions about the time, energy and skills of the volunteers that do not match the pool of available volunteers? Is communication of expectations clear from the start or muddled and vague, setting people up for failure?

9. *Do the Homework!* When assigning volunteers high level jobs of great importance, realize that such people are part of the staff in the sense that their responsibilities are critical to the success of the program. Check credentials carefully and ask for references from other managers who have worked with the volunteers previously. It is better to leave a position unfilled than to fill it with the first warm body through the door and have to pay the price for a misfit between volunteer and assignment at a later, more critical date.

There is no foolproof way for any manager to avoid having people lie to them. Fortunately it does not happen often, but when it does, it is in the best interests of all parties to deal with it quickly and effectively, with fairness and sensitivity. Understand that this becomes more difficult when the volunteer is embarrassed and emotionally fragile; it becomes less difficult though possibly more entangled when the lying was intentional and mean-spirited from the beginning.

Conflict Resolution and Negotiation

In handling problem volunteers, the volunteer director must have several skills that are critical to success. Primary among these skills are conflict resolution and deft negotiation.

There is not enough space here to go into great depth on the very complex subjects of conflict and negotiation; books that do are listed in the Bibliography, with the work of Elaine Yarbrough Ph.D. being the source of the learnings presented here. She has earned her reputation as the best and brightest on this topic!

Here are some basics that can be offered to help managers as they work to contain problems in their programs:

their programs:

1. Conflict is neither good nor bad. It simply is. It is the positive or negative reaction people offer when conflict arises that is critical.

2. Conflict generates energy. The challenge before the volunteer manager is to harness the energy for the good.

3. The goal of a conflict negotiation is to find resolution acceptable to those involved. The goal cannot be "win-lose", as any such "resolution" really means everyone loses.

4. To resolve conflicts, the real issues must be uncovered. Many times real issues are masked by symptoms or side issues. A volunteer may complain about not having a good parking space at the hospital but her real issue is she does not feel appreciated.

5. The volunteer manager must work toward problem-solving in a conflict without the impossible goal of making everyone 100% happy with the resolution. Resolution typically means compromise which allows those involved to get some, but not all, of what they want. Trying to make everyone happy is an Achilles heel among helping professionals and volunteer managers are no exception. Workers, either paid or volunteer or a combination of both, can work well together without being best buddies or agreeing on every point in life. Common goals can unite them.

Negotiating Peace
To bring about resolution to any conflict the volunteer manager must be adept at negotiating acceptable agreements. To begin this process there must be a clear understanding of two base

components in any conflict:

An *interest* is the issue a person has. It can be a desire, a concern, a goal, fear or need.

A *position* is the response or solution to a problem or concern; it is how a person reacts and the stand they take when a problem arises.

Issues or interests are an internal response. They are defined feelings that come because of an occurrence or stimulation; positions are what one chooses to do externally or overtly in response to what has happened. An example: A rumor spreads that the hospital volunteer department under pressure from some of its younger volunteers, is going to drop the uniforms (pink smocks) worn proudly for 23 years. Volunteer A immediately feels as though she will no longer be recognized for her hard work over 20 years! That's her issue or *Interest*.

Volunteer A responds by venting her anger and hurt at some younger volunteers whom she assumes started the movement to eliminate uniforms. She refuses to cooperate with them, tries to get others to reject them and speaks harshly to others about "the enemy." This is Volunteer A's *Position*.

As one might imagine, responses are governed greatly by the attitudes people have. It would be illogical to believe that a typically sour individual would respond positively when conflict arises; it is more likely that their response would reflect a more negative attitude in line with their usual sourness.

To truly reach an acceptable resolution to any conflict, the real issues or interest must be revealed. A clue that they are still lurking beneath what is being said comes when numerous attempts are made to move toward resolution and one or more of the parties involved continues to reject solutions and bring new complaints into the conversation.

The energy generated around conflict must be directed as much as possible away from negative responses which waste time and drain everyone. Recognize such negative drains when blaming others, defensiveness, rehashing old hurts, personal attacks or put-downs, score-keeping, overt or covert attempts to wound others or hysterical reactions to protect turf arise.

To negotiate good agreements that will stick and satisfy those involved, three areas must be addressed:

- Creating common ground.
- Loosening deadlocks.
- Creating specific expectations and consequences.

1. When *creating common ground*, effective negotiators are simply helping people focus on what they have in common. Often this has to do with a shared desire to assist clients or those who benefit from the volunteer program's efforts. A second commonality might be a desire to restore harmony among those working toward their shared goals.

In either case, a basis of agreement is sought so that those involved, no matter how dissimilar they may be, understand that they do have things in common. These commonalities become a "safe house" from which to find a conflict resolution and can be returned to when responses get out of control.

2. To *loosen deadlocks* where parties seem to have taken stands diametrically opposed to one another, the volunteer manager can choose one

or several strategies to relieve the tension of opposing demands:

- Find more areas that can offer an expanded win-win. Identify people's needs and explore ways to meet those needs. A volunteer may be insistent on keeping the traditional pink smock they've worn for their hospital volunteer corps for 20+ years but relax a bit when their need to be easily recognized in the facility is uncovered and a compromise reached by agreeing on an optional vest or armband that can be worn.

- Cut costs by finding out what is behind the resistance. Often the conflict is really about a volunteer feeling they would have to pay too high a "cost" if the change is implemented. To some volunteers the "cost" of not being recognized instantly in their hospital is far too high. Look for ways to reduce or eliminate costs.

- Compensate people for their cooperation so that there is a reward for their role in positive resolution of the conflict. "Would you help us design alternatives to the pink smock so that the options we offer our volunteers are most appealing?" Rewards might come in the way of public recognition, involvement in decisions, acclaim, direct help for a pet project, etc.

- Small concessions can help move toward resolution but usually only come after real issues have been identified, costs cut and compensation offered. At that point parties tend to relax a bit and are open to offering small concessions:

  "Well I will admit some of the younger volunteers do look a bit silly in a pink smock; I can see how they might like the option of no uniform at all."

  And from the opposition:

  "I can understand how some of the volunteers who began this program 20 years ago have seen the smock as an outward symbol of their importance to the hospital. I can see why they would appreciate the option of wearing something that is easily recognizable by everyone. It's really a badge of honor."

- Bridging is the identification of a middle

ground as evidenced in the example noted above. The focus then moves from "Pink Smocks Forever!" versus "Down With Pink Smocks!" to a redesigned, optional article people might or might not choose to wear. Who knows, those opposed may even suggest that those volunteers wishing to retain their pinks might just be allowed to do so, without mandating newer volunteers to follow suit! The pink smock then designates a founding or long-term volunteer.

In a highly complex conflict well beyond the more simplistic issue of smocks, it may be wise to take small steps toward resolution. If two organizations are hoping to merge, for example, it is almost guaranteed that parties from each will object to a perceived loss of autonomy and control (the COST of merger). The real issue may be trust and control, thus the wise negotiator sets up small steps of getting parties from each group together so they can begin to build trust as they get to know one another.

It is also critical in resolving conflicts to know what to do if the negotiation gets "stuck." If that happens the good negotiator knows that they should ask those involved to step back and find a way to set acceptable criteria (i.e., "Neither group will make decisions that impact both without consulting the other.") or acceptable process (i.e., "We will meet a week from today, each bringing three people who will form a joint resolution committee."). In both examples, the goal of the negotiator is to help people step back into safe areas of non-conflict and take even smaller steps toward agreements.

3. The third area of good agreements is the agreement it self which needs to be *specific and measurable with consequences* spelled out should the contract be broken. Fluff statements such as "We all agree to get along and work harmoniously" should be avoided at all costs. Leave nothing to interpretation. Spell out who does what, when, where and how. Attach timelines, list ultimate goals and make them measurable. Draw up lines of authority, responsibility and even the handling of grievances so that everyone involved knows who to turn to when questions arise. Discuss ways to handle any fine-

tuning the agreement might need in the future. Spell out any legal or financial issues most carefully and with expert advice.

Do not forget the all important aspect of recognition as those people who hammered out the resolution and those who make it work are openly rewarded and praised. This will not only thank those who used their energies positively and helped to bring peace to a program, but will model behavior that can be repeated in the future.

Evaluating Volunteers
One of the necessary requirements for dealing with disruptive volunteers is a system for evaluating their performance. The system must both look at each volunteer's performance and contain a way to adjust their performance toward the better. It must also be helpful in working with volunteers who are not disruptive, but who simply need assistance in becoming even better than they currently are.

The prospect of conducing an evaluation of a volunteer is not commonly one that is looked forward to with great enthusiasm by most volunteer managers, or by staff who work with volunteers. Many volunteer programs, in truth, cannot even claim to have a process for volunteer evaluation, except in a very loose sense. Evaluation, however, is not something to be avoided, especially if you realize that it can actually be a very positive management device.

Why Evaluate Volunteers?
Rather than dreading the prospect of evaluation, the smart volunteer supervisor should realize two important facts:

- Most volunteers want to do the best job that they can. The absence of feedback and assistance is both demeaning and disturbing to them.

- Most volunteers will "win" in assessment situations.

Failing to evaluate a volunteer sends a clear message that you don't care about the quality of the work being done, and that you don't care much about the volunteer. Both volunteers who know they aren't doing well and those who think they should be congratulated for good work will think less of the volunteer effort, and of you, if evaluations are not conducted.

There are two basic reasons for conducting a volunteer evaluation:

1. To help the volunteer work closer to their potential.

2. To help the organization better involve volunteers.

And there is one key reason for not conducting evaluations: To deal with all the small performance problems that supervisors have been ignoring since the last evaluation.

A periodic volunteer evaluation can help shape the overall performance of the volunteer, but it cannot and should not replace the day-to-day on-site coaching and supervision that must occur.

Setting Up the Evaluation System
There are a number of ways to develop an evaluation system. The first issue to be faced is what to call it. Here are some possibilities:

* Evaluation system
* Performance assessment system
* Work appraisal
* Progress planning
* Feedback

Clearly these have different connotations. Our suggestion is that you call the system by the same terminology as is used for paid staff, since this will send a clear message about job equality. You should also attempt to make the processes of the system congruent, if not identical, to that utilized with staff.

Whatever system you create should contain the following elements:

* A policy on performance appraisal and review.

* An initial trial period for all volunteers, before they are officially accepted and enrolled by the agency.

* A system for developing and maintaining current and accurate job descriptions for each volunteer.

* A periodic scheduled evaluation meeting between the volunteer and their supervisor to discuss job performance and satisfaction.

* A method for reviewing commitments to change made during the evaluation meeting.

This system should be explained to each volunteer during their initial orientation session, and should be reviewed with each staff person who will be supervising volunteers.

It All Starts with the Job Description
It is impossible to conduct good evaluations if you do not have accurate job descriptions for each volunteer. Remember Lynch's Law: "Lousy job descriptions produce really lousy evaluation sessions." Without a good job description which outlines the goals, objectives, and performance measures of the job, the supervisor will not know what they are asking of the volunteer and the volunteer will not know what is expected them. Remember McCurley's Rule of Thumb: "If you don't know what you want from the volunteer, why should they?"

The most difficult part of this effort is getting supervisors to change the job descriptions of volunteers as time passes. You can encourage this by having them re-write the descriptions after each evaluation session, or as part of each annual planning session (making the jobs match the new strategic efforts of the department or program).

Conducting the Evaluation
The evaluation session should be a two-way meeting. It is your chance to talk about the volunteer's performance, giving either praise or suggestions for improvement. It should also be the volunteer's opportunity to talk about how

Handling Problem Volunteers

their participation can be enhanced, which might even include discussing their moving to a new volunteer position.

The easiest method of conducting the evaluation session is to follow the RAP method:

- Review the past.

- Analyze the present.

- Plan the future.

And here are some suggestions:

1.   *Don't get overwhelmed by forms.* The main purpose of the session is to have a substantive conversation with the volunteer about how their volunteering can be improved, not to simply fill out forms for the filing system. The forms are helpful (and can particularly be so for your poor successor who may be trying desperately to find out what went on before she got there), but they are not the major concern during the discussion. The forms do become a more important concern when you are attempting to correct disruptive behavior because they will become your record of what steps are planned by the volunteer to correct problems. Forms can also become useful as a record for terminating the volunteer's relationship with the agency, as we will address in the next chapter.

2.   *Start with the job description.* Begin by finding out if it in fact describes what the volunteer has been doing. Take notes so you can adjust it closer to reality. The major 'problem' with highly motivated volunteers is that they produce rapid 'scope creep' in their assignments. You don't want to discourage this, but you do want to know about it.

3.   *Stick to the basics*: job proficiency, working relationships, comparison with last review.

4.   *Listen as least as much as you talk.* When you schedule the session with the volunteer, tell them this is their opportunity to evaluate the volunteer program and you want their ideas on how to make things better both for them and for other volunteers.

5.   *Don't forget that the street goes both ways.* Remember that the evaluation may show as much what you need to do as it does what the volunteer needs to do.

Reprimanding

If the evaluation does deal with some unsatisfactory performance by the volunteer, follow these simple guidelines when giving a reprimand:

1.   *Don't smile.* This is a serious subject, and you will simply confuse the volunteer if you are saying one thing and acting in a different manner.

2.   *Don't gunny sack*; i.e. don't save up a lot of small criticisms and drop them all on the volunteer at the same time. These should be dealt with in smaller segments during regular volunteer/supervisor conversations.

3.   *Be specific.* Talk about what the volunteer is not doing in the way you want them to. Avoid vague comments, particularly if they are about the volunteer's attitude or motivations as opposed to the volunteer's action or behavior.

4.   *Let the volunteer know how you feel.* Indicate that both you and program expect quality performance and that you are disappointed by the unsatisfactory work.

5.   *Put the reprimand in perspective.* If the volunteer has done good work in other areas or at other times, remind them of that good performance.

6.   *Don't repeat the reprimand.* Cover the area that needs improvement and move on.

It is important to consider the possibility that the reprimand will not solve your problem. You would optimistically like to think so, and in many cases minor corrective action can achieve positive results. In case, however, that problems do continue, it is important to begin developing a case history of the problem situation. This case history will be important both in tracking what you are doing to correct the problem and also to develop a record of the problem for use if more harsh measures become necessary..

Following the reprimand, write a memo to the file that indicates the following:

- The specific facts of the incident, including dates, parties involved, and the specific nature of the misperformance for which the reprimand was given.

- The nature of the conversation with the volunteer about the incident or situation, including their own explanation of the reasons for their performance.

- Any corrective actions that were identified with the volunteer, including any timeline for their implementation.

While regrettable, this will both help you to determine what you need to do and potentially establish for others the history of the situation.

Conclusion

These types of volunteers are a question mark - they may be savable and they may not. They may be worth the effort of re-directing and they may be more trouble than they're worth.

The goal of the manager is to identify which are worth the effort and to determine how these volunteers can be returned to productivity.

Chapter Five
The Dangerously
Dysfunctional Volunteer

Introduction

Some problem volunteer situations are so extreme that the only possible method for dealing with them is to remove the volunteer from the agency as quickly as possible. In this chapter we deal with some varieties of this type of situation and with establishing and implementing a system for terminating unsuitable volunteers.

The Emotionally Disturbed Volunteer

- *Defendant was convicted of reckless endangerment in the second degree (Penal Law §120.20), a class A misdemeanor, after a jury trial. Defendant, a hospital volunteer, disconnected the life support of an AIDS patient in the belief that he had been healed by prayer.* People v. Lena Tychanski, 78 N.Y.2d 909 (1991).

- *Sacramento - A former Suicide Prevention Center volunteer confessed he slit the wrists of a chronic caller who had become too demanding, according to testimony in an attempted murder case.*

  Frank Charles Snyder, 29, admitted that he and an acquaintance who has been identified only as John had attacked a depressed and suicidal Benjamin Carlson on February 12, sheriff's Sgt Joseph Dean testified Wednesday.

  Carlson, who survived, "was sucking everything out of me...he antagonized me so that I would kill him," Dean quoted Snyder as saying. Associated Press, May 24, 1991

Roughly 100 million people volunteer in this country, so it should be no surprise that some of them are mentally unbalanced. This may express itself in related behaviors (alcoholism, drug abuse, etc.) or it may express itself directly (crime, sexual assault). It may even express itself in behaviors that are more harmful to the person involved rather than others, as in the emotionally disturbed volunteer.

In recent years many volunteer programs have intentionally begun working with volunteers who are transitioning from a personal crisis, utilizing volunteering as a bridge. This is a noble and often rewarding effort, and if you are interested in assisting you should read John Weaver's *Working with Volunteers Who Are Mentally Ill.*

It is also possible, however, to have a volunteer in your problem whose psychological state makes them a danger to others.

Part of this danger may be purposeful in nature, such as theft or abuse. It can be particularly frightful because it is often deliberately concealed, with the act of volunteering used as a means of gaining access to victims. Volunteer programs which work with clientele of diminished capacities (children, seniors, those with disabilities) need to be especially cautious in determining this type of behavior during the screening process. The upsurge in criminal record checks of potential volunteers has been fueled by abuse situations involving volunteers. Another protective method is imposition of a requirement that volunteers never be in unsupervised or unaccompanied situations with clients, especially children.

Many psychological problems may be unintentional in nature, but may still potentially render the volunteer unfit for service. The difficulty in dealing with these situations is that they commonly require a degree of knowledge and expertise beyond that held by most volunteer managers.

Here are some suggestions for dealing with these situations:

1. Use the interviewing process to screen for potential problems. One of the questions to ask of potential volunteers is, "Are you under any

course of treatment that might affect your ability to do volunteer work?" The intent of this question is not to arbitrarily deny a volunteer position to anyone who responds "yes," but rather to open a dialogue about what the condition being treated is and how it might affect volunteering, and what the agency might do to make volunteering more effective. The intent is to protect both the agency and the potential volunteer.

2. If the condition being treated is one which the volunteer manager does not completely understand, is one that seems to impose some dangers or limitations, or is one whose severity is difficult to estimate, then the best thing to do is to involve the treating physician in the discussion. They, after all, have the greatest familiarity with the patient and their condition. Ask the potential volunteer to have their physician review the job description for which the volunteer is applying and give their approval as to the safety and suitability of the placement. If the physician is reluctant to do so, then you should be reluctant as well.

3. Take more care in your initial training and placement of the volunteer. This may involve creating a "buddy" system in which a partner volunteer simultaneously supports and monitors the newcomer. This additional assistance may eliminate future problems and may greatly ease the transition process.

If a problem arises despite these efforts, then you should try to refer the volunteer to professional counseling. In a larger organization you may even have access to an employee counseling system which can be opened to volunteers. While at the same time you are following steps discussed earlier to alter the volunteer performance you should also be helping the volunteer to seek assistance which can help deal with the causes of the problem, and which is clearly beyond what most supervisors should be involved in providing personally.

The Organizational Terrorist
There is a new, subtle and sadly potent weapon

being used effectively by many employees and some volunteers who are desperate to keep their positions in the face of evidence that they are not suited for the work assigned them.

Their weapon is a threat of a suit against the individuals who have called them to task in regard to their performance. To strengthen their hand, they extend their threat to suggesting that they will also bring suit against the organization in which they work, thus escalating the conflict to the highest and most potent level.

All of this is a subtle extension of the age-old response of shooting the messenger, and it is being used more and more as desperate people adopt desperate measures to hang on to jobs that afford them security, status or power.

This is a true story:

A program director of a large, state-wide organization, had a grievance suit filed against her by a paid worker she supervised. The worker claimed the director had "harassed her daily, thus causing mental anguish; had discriminated against her and had withheld necessary information which was needed to successfully do her job."

The director had to gather evidence to prove that the worker had not had critical information withheld and that the "harassment" she contended was a series of meetings between them in which behavior (coming to work late, inappropriate language, etc.) and job performance (completing assignments, following direct instructions, lying about results, etc.) was discussed along with corrective efforts the employee agreed to take.

The director's legal department assured her that she has no need to be concerned because she had documented contacts and corrective actions in writing, however, "It still worries me to death, because anything can happen" she related.

This was the third suit in 18 months(two from paid staff, one from a key volunteer) within her department and she estimated that the new suit would take about 1/4th of her time and energy each week. She is determined to see it through but has also come to the conclusion that when it is disposed of, she will leave her position.

"I have no more stomach or energy to spend my time fighting such unfair tactics let alone having to constantly work around and clean up after this employee's poor work," she stated.

A small but growing number of such cases have arisen in the past few years where poor-performance workers, paid or non-paid, have threatened or actually brought legal actions against individuals/groups in an effort to retain their positions.

There can be no dispute that legal recourse in legitimate cases of grievance is necessary for workers who have truly been abused, but all too many people who are looking for a tool to cover their ineptitude and hang on to their jobs have found the same protection a weapon for organizational terrorism.

As the number of cases of the negative use of legal recourse grows, so also do the number of good people who, as in this example, find it "not worth it" to stay connected to an organization which is too easily cowered by such threats. They choose to relocate in one which will not give into such tactics.

In discussing the issue of legal liabilities of such incidents volunteer managers have discovered that there are some organizations which employ a staff member who works exclusively to investigate and try to mediate such disputes. The employee's mandate is to swiftly correct legitimate claims of harassment and discrimination through immediate reprimand of the offender and on-going monitoring but to also identify those suits which are being brought unfairly in an effort to cover worker incompetence, illegal actions, impropriety or fraud.

All of the stories encountered in examining this issue have common threads even when the specific facts of the cases are unique. Such destructive corporate terrorism, which threatens explosive consequences to individuals and organizations, seems to be characterized by at least one of the following:

1. The worker, paid or volunteer, uses the threat of a grievance suit to protect their position.

2. They are typically attempting to divert attention from their own inappropriate behavior or performance.

3. They have typically had a long-standing record of being confronted with specific examples of poor performance.

4. They have demonstrated a pattern of blaming others for failures in their own job performance.

5. Colleagues have brought specific examples of poor performance by the worker to their supervisor; complaints are not coming from a single person, but several.

6. The more a supervisor attempts to work with the person to point out specific problems and design corrective action, the more defensive the worker becomes. There is a response of: "You're picking on me. You won't let me do my job!"

7. Often their personal behavior reflects problems that parallel work behavior patterns: a worker who seems unable to make decisions in their job assignments is also noticed to be unable to make decisions in their personal life; workers who have trouble concentrating on job skills also demonstrate an inability to concentrate in their off-work life.

8. Often, when confronted with specific mistakes they have made, they have a ready excuse designed to divert criticism. Many times such excuses are shrouded in "feel sorry for me" stories:

"I've had health problems;" "I am having to deal with terrible stress in my family life;" "I hadn't wanted to report this but a co worker has been making my life miserable...I won't say who it is, because I don't want to make any trouble for our wonderful work family, but it has really drained my energies and diverted me from doing an excellent job;" and they can get even more creative!

Handling Problem Volunteers

9. Among the most cunning - and dangerous - workers who resort to legal terrorism, are those people who are very skilled at getting other people to do their work for them ("You always have such good ideas, could you outline how you think this should be handled?"), or hiding behind process ("Before we take action let's do a study and then integrate responses into a think-tank session of brain-storming and putting our thoughts in grid patterns for behavior analysis." Huh?).

They can also be masters of the "poor bad me; I'm unworthy to be in your company" ploy. With this strategy, they turn on themselves verbally in such an over-blown fashion that the person who is attempting to reprimand them becomes fearful that they will destroy themselves and therefore shifts into a rescuer, "Now, now, don't be so hard on yourself" mode. It goes like this:

Supervisor: *"Worker, it's come to my attention that you did not get our grant proposal into the XYZ Foundation in time to meet their deadline. You had promised me faithfully that this was not going to happen again this year as it did last. I'm very disappointed in this inaction, as it means that we have lost the possibility of some critical funding. It also forces me to put you on termination notice."*

Worker: *"Supervisor you have every right to be angry with me. I knew how important it was to get the proposal in on time and it was actually ready before the deadline but I was so overwhelmed with some terrible problems at home that I had the wrong date in my mind and simply blew it. I love this organization so much and I'm simply doubting my abilities; I know its because of the terrible stress I'm*

under...I can't sleep, I can't eat, sometimes I even have trouble getting out of bed in the morning. I think sometimes I just cant face another day of failure. You have every right to fire me; I'm no good to you or myself this way. When I went to my neighbor's funeral several months ago I actually envied him the peace of mind he must feel; I'm certainly no good to anyone the way I feel these days...I'm sorry, I'm not making sense..."*

Supervisor: *"Now, now, let's not make this larger than it really is. I believe you may need to speak to a mental health professional. We'll simply put the issue of the grant proposal on hold until you've had a chance to get some help."*

Worker: *"I really thank you, Supervisor, you've given me hope again."* (...and to themselves, the crafty manipulator: "*Gottcha.*")

So How Does One Protect Themselves Against Such Terrorism?
There is no foolproof way to avoid such tactics of workers who are either unscrupulous, unstable or deeply insecure, however, one or more of the following measures might help:

1. Try to avoid placing such folks in the first place. That of course is easier said than done, but people who are going to be quick to turn to legal terrorism typically have displayed this propensity before. Check each new employment or high-level volunteer applicant very carefully. If you see a pattern of leaving jobs on a regular basis, don't rely on letters of recommendations alone, call previous supervisors or see them in person. Guarantee strict confidence in asking for any hidden reason the person in question really left their previous job.

Specifically ask if any legal actions were associated with the worker and watch their body language or listen for a change in voice tones when this subject is broached. Even if they deny such concerns or reply they cannot divulge such information, is there a "feeling" that a hot spot has been touched?

It is interesting to note that several employers who are experiencing difficulty with current employees or volunteers have gone back to past supervisors and uncovered a behavior pattern of threatening legal actions to cover work inadequacies. Typically when such previous employers have been bluntly asked why they gave the worker a recommendation, they just as bluntly

2. When promoting someone from within a very large organization, check carefully to insure that the current supervisor is not "pushing" the new placement because they want them out from under also! Most co-workers are very careful about leveling any criticism toward a colleague (often for fear of a grievance suit themselves), but will signal in some manner their concerns even if they don't give specifics.

Managers are urged to listen to their gut instincts. If something doesn't feel right, pursue its roots until satisfied that the true nature of the people being considered as part of the work team has been uncovered. The hair on the back of one's neck may be the best tool in identifying workers who will later cause great grief and energy drains.

3. Make sure that several people interview candidates for critical job assignments. Do not hand over the screening process to the personnel department. Have several layers of interviewing - an initial screening by a person-nel worker, a departmental worker's interview for skill-specific screening, a potential co-worker interview to focus on a specific job and a supervisor interview to determine final placement and how such a can-didate might fit into a work team in their department.

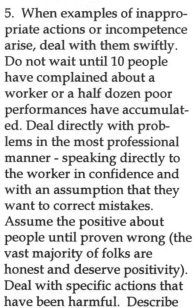

Have these people then compare notes. Talk about specific skills and assign-ments AND gut feelings about a person. Make sure that a thorough background check has been accomplished and weigh the different perspectives of those involved as the feasibility of bringing the person on board is determined.

4. Without spreading a panic of paranoia, make sure that part of orientation of new workers includes instructions on carefully documenting behavior of all kinds. Train supervisors in ways to positively correct inappropriate behavior including having another person present when specific actions are being discussed and correc-tive action is being explained.

This serves several purposes:

a. It trains supervisors and co-workers in appropriate, positive corrective procedures.

b. It announces to all workers that methods are in place to thwart legal terrorism.

c. It provides proof that could be used in grievance hearings that the organization has processes designed to help workers correct inappropriate behavior for both paid and volunteer workers.

d. It offers workers instruction on filing grievances, thus putting everyone on notice that legitimate offenses will be dealt with promptly. This also provides proof of the organization's good faith in providing processes for legitimate grievances.

5. When examples of inappro-priate actions or incompetence arise, deal with them swiftly. Do not wait until 10 people have complained about a worker or a half dozen poor performances have accumulat-ed. Deal directly with prob-lems in the most professional manner - speaking directly to the worker in confidence and with an assumption that they want to correct mistakes. Assume the positive about people until proven wrong (the vast majority of folks are honest and deserve positivity). Deal with specific actions that have been harmful. Describe specific consequences of this action or behavior. Avoid "soft" statements that attack personally - talk about what happened because a report was not in on time rather than "you never follow directions." Be specific and document the con-versation. Follow up in written form to the worker and ask them to acknowledge the receipt of this documentation that will be kept in their confidential personnel file. If negative repercussions are suspected, openly tape record sessions.

When Threats of Suits Come, How To Respond?
The trickiest part may come in honestly listen-ing to complaints being leveled and determin-ing their legitimacy. It needs to be determined:

Handling Problem Volunteers

a. Is this a real case of harassment? Do the facts bear witness to its reality? Is the person doing the complaining believable? Are there specific incidents being reported? If so do everything to verify them and then deal with the root problem and the individuals involved, hopefully without having to take it into a hearing or court.

b. If the facts just don't ring true, work to determine if the accuser is:

- aware that their performance is unacceptable and trying to divert attention from their actions by pointing the finger at their accuser, saying "They made me do it,!" or

- unaware that their performance is below par and feeling it must be someone else's fault, or

- simply wanting to get someone else in trouble (yes, there are such people), possibly because they feel their status or position is threatened or they feel someone is about to uncover some information the complaining worker is trying to keep covered up or they feel the need to get a person "back" for some previous, perceived slight.

Sadly, yes, this does happen. A church secretary had for several years found creative ways to get rid of volunteers assigned to help her with record keeping. She tried to simply make life so miserable for them they either left or did her bidding which removed them from looking at records regarding Sunday School collections. When she ran into two volunteers who would not be intimidated by her approach, she went to the Pastor to complain of their harassment and breaking rules of confidentiality. When this happened the second time, the Pastor became suspicious, insisted that he would be assisting for a week or two and was not terribly surprised when she did everything she could to insist that wasn't necessary, he would "get in her way", and finally (no surprise!) he was now "harassing" her too.

Of course, his inspection disclosed that she had been skimming contributions, and when confronted with the evidence, can you guess what she did? Hired a lawyer to sue the church and Pastor for harassment and framing her! The suit was dismissed when she finally confessed, but in the meantime, everyone suffered!

Another type of person who threatens legal action against an individual and their parent organization is the most difficult to deal with. This is the person who, at some level, knows they are trying to divert attention from inadequacies, but at a conscious level actually believes their failures are the fault of someone else.

Such a person is typically fragile and terribly desperate. Often they are intelligent, creative, good-souled people who have simply found themselves in over their head. They have every intention of doing a good job and often work long hours trying to do what is expected of them. The harder they work and the more hours they put in, however, the more confused and dysfunctional they become.

It is like many people who have gone to the store and purchased a computer, brought it home with a determination to "become computer literate", set it up and then become totally frustrated trying to make different software behave properly. They learn enough to get by, but when real understanding is required to do their bidding, they become more and more frustrated, often blaming the computer for errors. They refer to manuals but find them written in gibberish; they ask others who explain in such rapid-fire instructions that they miss critical information; they feel less and less adequate and greater anger at that #@!!**# machine.

It is not, of course, the machines fault. It's also not theirs. It is simply a matter of not being equipped to use the computer successfully. They are in over their head, out of their element and sadly, feeling very inadequate.

Should it be suspected that this is the case with a paid or volunteer worker who goes on and on about how someone else has harassed or sabotaged them, it is important to listen carefully, documenting all specifics and then discussing their assignment with them. Offer solutions that would remove them from the assignment that seems to be at the base of their problems to try to de-escalate the conflict. Seek a new assignment in the organization that would tap their skills and remove them from the pain of having to remain "in over their heads", as their threatened actions may then be avoided.

This method will NOT work with people who are threatening actions because they are mean-spirited or truly deceitful. It can work with good people who have simply become desperate and are looking for a way to save face while getting out of jobs that do not match their skill level.

The Cost of Terrorism

It is almost impossible to really assess the cost of such terrorist tactics to organizations or individuals. There are of course legal fees that can be tabulated, but such figures don't truly measure the hidden costs.

How, for example, can anyone measure the exhaustion people experience when they are the brunt of such terrorist tactics? It takes enormous energies to defend against unfounded and unfair attacks. When a person must fight to prove their innocence, it reduces the energies they have to also do their job, thus costing clients, colleagues and the organization potential effectiveness.

Going back to the first example, how does anyone measure the loss of those people who decide it is no longer worth it to fight such re-occurring battles and who simply resign when they can?

At some point, every person wounded by the shrapnel of such terrorism makes a choice of fight or flight, weighing the pain and frustration against the benefits of continued association.

The best and brightest of paid staff and volunteers simply decide "who needs this?" and move on to offer their talents elsewhere when they are forced to make-do around the incompetence of people the organization is afraid to remove for fear of legal repercussions.

Time, energy, creatively, financial and public support, information and enthusiasm are often lost in the fallout of the terrorism used by many to protect their positions and deflect attention from their inadequacies. How can such costs be measured? They can't, except to realize that it is more than any organization can afford.

Firing the Problem Volunteer

One of the recurrent nightmares of any volunteer manager is encountering a situation in which they may have to consider 'firing' a volunteer. For many this prospect creates severe stress, both over the appropriateness of the action and over fear of possible legal and political consequences. Ann Cook, in a survey of Foster Grandparents Programs in 23 communities discovered that 82% of responding volunteer managers rated the decision to terminate a volunteer as being a 'difficult or very difficult issue' for them. Over 60% of the volunteer directors reported delaying dealing with the issue when they encountered it.

Getting Philosophically Ready

The initial requirement in developing a system for handling volunteer termination decisions is to decide that firing volunteers is, in general, a potentially appropriate action. Over the years this has been a difficult issue for many individual coordinators to address, probably because they are very people-oriented and appreciate the willingness of others to help in their programs. These coordinators have had particular difficulty in dealing with situations in which the decision to terminate was not due to any particular 'fault' on the part of the volunteer, but was instead due to ill health or a change in program needs. Programs in which there have been a focus on volunteering as a benefit to the volunteer (such as most of ACTION's Older American Volunteer Programs) have also had great difficulty with this issue because they classify volunteers as 'clients' of the program, and it is philosophically difficult to justify terminating a client.

Handling Problem Volunteers

An agency which contemplates firing volunteers may adopt several philosophical justifications. One is simply that the bottom line is the ability to deliver quality service to the clients of the agency and any barrier to that delivery is not allowable. This standard would apply to both paid and unpaid staff, as Jane Mallory Park points out: "Whether the personnel in question are paid or volunteer, it is important to have policies and practices which promote accountability and the highest levels of performance possible without ignoring the reality that all individuals have idiosyncrasies and limitations as well as strengths. A double standard which does not give respect and dignity to both volunteers and paid staff is not only unnecessary but is also unhealthy for individuals and organizations."

A second philosophical approach has to do with giving meaning and value to volunteer service. By denying that there is a 'right' and a 'wrong' way to do a volunteer job, one conveys the impression that the volunteer work done is irrelevant and insignificant. An agency which does not care enough about the work done by volunteers to enforce quality communicates to other volunteers that the agency believes their own work to be meaningless.

The philosophical decision by an agency to fire volunteers is one that should be addressed prior to any incident. It should be discussed and ratified by staff and then codified as part of the overall policy statement on volunteer utilization and included as part of the agency's volunteer policies

Looking for Alternatives to Firing
Before addressing development of a system for firing volunteers, it is important to note that the decision to terminate a volunteer should always be, in practice, a reluctant last resort.

Firing a volunteer is an admission that volunteer management has failed. It means that the interviewing system did not work, or the job design was faulty, or that training and supervision did not operate the way it should. It is as much an indictment of the agency as it is of the volunteer.

And it is crucial to remember that many situations that appear to warrant firing may actually be remediable by less stringent methods. Before contemplating firing a volunteer, see if any of the following approaches may be more appropriate and less painful:

• *Re-Supervise*. You may have a volunteer who doesn't understand that the rules of the agency have to be followed. This is a common problem for agencies who utilize youth volunteers, some of whom automatically 'test' the rules as part of their self-expression. Re-enforcement may end the problem.

• *Re-Assign*. Transfer the volunteer to a new position. You may, on the basis of a short interview, have misread their skills or inclinations. They may simply not be getting along with the staff or other volunteers with whom they are working. Try them in a new setting and see what happens.

• *Re-Train*. Send them back for a second education. Some people take longer than others to learn new techniques. Some may require a different training approach, such as one-on-one mentoring rather than classroom lectures. If the problem is lack of knowledge rather than lack of motivation, then work to provide the knowledge.

• *Re-Vitalize*. If a long-time volunteer has started to malfunction, they may just need a rest. This is particularly true with volunteers who have intense jobs, such as one-to-one work with troubled clients. The volunteer may not realize or admit that they're burned out. Give them a sabbatical and let them re-charge. Practice 'crop rotation' and transfer them temporarily to something that is less emotionally draining.

• *Refer*. Maybe they just need a whole new outlook of life, one they can only get by volunteering in an entirely different agency. Refer them to the Volunteer Center or set up an exchange program with a sister agency. Swap your volunteers for a few months and let them learn a few new tricks.

• *Retire*. Recognize that some volunteers may simply reach a diminished capacity in which they can no longer do the work they once did and may even be a danger to themselves and to others. Give them the honor they deserve and ensure that they don't end their volunteer careers in a way they will regret. Assist them in departing with dignity before the situation becomes a tragic crisis.

All of these alternatives are both easier to implement and managerially smarter than making a decision to terminate a volunteer. They recognize that there are many reasons why a person may be behaving inappropriately and that some of these reasons have answers other than separating that person from the program. We strongly urge that you consider each of these alternatives before deciding to fire any volunteer.

Developing a System for Making Firing Decisions

If you do, however, encounter a situation in which none of the alternatives work, it is helpful to have in place a system for dealing with problems. Some agencies have been sued by terminated volunteers and many agencies have encountered political and community relations problems. The system that follows is designed to help the volunteer manager both in making and in justifying the decision to terminate a volunteer. Essentially, it has three parts:

1. Forewarning/Notice

The first stage of the system is developing clear policies and information about the prospect of firing volunteers. To actualize these, an agency needs to develop the following:

• A set of official policies regarding volunteer personnel issues. It is especially important to have policies on probation, suspension, and termination. We've provided some examples of possible policies in Chapter 6.

• A system for informing volunteers, in advance, about the policies. This would include a planned orientation system which discusses the policies and provides examples of requirements and

unacceptable behavior. It would also include regularly conducted evaluation sessions in which plans and expectations for future activities are discussed and agreed to.

• A way of relating the policies to each volunteer job. This means having a job description for the volunteer which explains the requirements of the job for which the volunteer has been accepted, and has some measurable objectives for determining whether the work was accomplished. The most common transgression of this requirement is the volunteer whose position has "grown" or "mutated" over the years, but no one has bothered to update their job description.

2. Investigation/Determination

The second part of the system involves developing a process for determining whether the volunteer has actually broken the rules. This implies having a fair investigator take the time to examine the situation and reach a determination that something has been done wrongly.

This means, by the way, that one should never terminate a volunteer "on the spot," regardless of the infraction. "Instant firing" doesn't allow one to determine whether there are extenuating circumstances. This is why a suspension or probation policy is so important.

Essentially, in this part of the system the volunteer manager needs to establish a process for reviewing the behavior of volunteers and recording problems. On an on-going basis this should be done as part of the regular evaluation process for volunteers. Those volunteers whose performance is unsatisfactory are told of their deficiency, counseled on improving their work, and then re-evaluated. Failure to conform to the quality standard over time becomes grounds for termination. In cases where the wrongful performance is not incremental, but is substantial in nature (inappropriate relations

Handling Problem Volunteers

with a client or breach of confidentiality) then what is needed is some 'proof' that the volunteer did in fact commit the wrong-doing. This might be testimony of other volunteers, staff, or the client.

Another element to investigate during this phase is how the agency has handled similar situations in the past, both involving this volunteer and others.

During this part of the process the volunteer manager also investigates whether any of the alternatives to firing would be a more appropriate solution. The keys during this process are to not be hasty, to get all the facts, and to be as objective and unemotional as possible.

3. Application
This final part of the system requires that the volunteer manager do a fair job of enforcing the system. It requires equal and fair application of the rules (no playing favorites), appropriate penalties (graduated to the severity of the offense) and, if possible, a review process, so that the decision does not look like a personal one.

You will note that the above three processes mirror the common personnel practices for paid staff. They are, in fact, the same, and they should be, since evaluating either paid or unpaid staff should follow the same rules.

The advantages of this system are two-fold. First, they assist the volunteer manager in making the right decision, and in feeling comfortable about making that decision. The system is fair to both the volunteer and the agency if properly followed and tends to produce 'correct' answers. It also allows the volunteer manager to divert to a less drastic solution as appropriate.

Second, the system helps develop a case for firing that can be utilized to explain the decision to others, whether internally or externally. You will need the support of other staff within your agency before implementing this type of solution, particularly if the volunteer involved

has some stature in the agency or the community. In practice, in fact, an odd side-effect of this systematic approach is that many problem volunteers decide to voluntarily resign rather than face the inevitable and seemingly inexorable conclusion of the process. Most people prefer not to sit in front of an oncoming train...

The steps above may be slightly different in various organizations. 4-H, for example, has a system which involves four ascending steps:

1. an official warning letter to the volunteer indicating specific information or areas that need improvement

2. follow-up counseling along with a letter of documentation

3. probation with explicit goals

4. termination

If the decision is made that the conduct of the volunteer warrants termination, then the clear duty of the volunteer manager is to implement the decision. In the words of Jane Mallory Park, "Certain behaviors by paid or volunteer personnel cannot be tolerated by a responsible organization: outright harm to clients; inappropriate public statements; flagrant and willful violation of policies and procedures; etc. If a person's performance is irredeemably inadequate or if his/her attitudes are so recalcitrant and disruptive that the morale of other personnel is understandably low, what is really gained by permitting the situation to drag on?"

Documenting the Case for Termination
While lawsuits by volunteers against organizations for termination are rare, it is increasingly essential to make sure that you not only have a good reason for firing a volunteer, but also have the documentation to establish the validity of that reason to others. Key elements in this documentation are:

1. Records of the deficiencies in the volunteer's performance, giving as precise a description as possible of specific, observable behavior of the volunteer which violates agency rules or procedures.

2. Written records of the times you speak to the volunteer about their conduct or performance, with indications of the steps they agree to take to correct the problem and notes on the timeframe for any change in behavior.

3. Records of statements by others about the conduct or performance of the volunteers, preferably signed by the person giving the testimony.

4. Records of the steps in the evaluation and assessment process, including warnings to the volunteer, performance agreements, formal evaluation forms, etc.

Make sure that the volunteer receives copies of all communications which are directed to them, but it is not necessary to give the volunteer a copy of memorandum that you write to the personnel file or to others about their behavior.

You may discover behavior which would prompt you to dismiss a volunteer, but in reviewing their personnel file notice that all other documentation about their past behavior is either missing or else contains no criticism. In this case, you should be cautious, and take the time to see whether tough action is warranted. This is one of the occasions when new volunteer managers have been justified in cursing their predecessors, who may have left them with a problem but with no personnel file to indicate its extent or duration, or to help build a case for dismissing the problem volunteer.

Conducting the Firing Meeting

Regardless of the system utilized to reach the decision to terminate, someone has to actually convey that decision to the volunteer. This will never be a pleasant experience, but here are some tips which may help:

1. *Conduct the meeting in a private setting.* This will preserve the dignity of the volunteer and perhaps of yourself. You may choose to have one additional staff person present to witness the procedure, by make sure you know what each of you will be saying and not saying during the conversation. The role of the third person should primarily be to listen as a neutral witness. They should not be anyone who is currently involved in supervising or working with the volunteer. You may also want to have the meeting in a neutral setting, other than the supervisor's office.

2. *Be quick, direct, and absolute.* Don't beat around the bush. It is quite embarrassing to have the volunteer show up for work the next day because they didn't get the hint. Practice the exact words you will use in telling the volunteer, and make sure they are unequivocal. Do not back down from them even if you want to preserve your image as a 'nice person'. Have a written notice of termination to present to the volunteer. It should review the disciplinary history and events leading to the termination and list procedures (such as turning in badges or uniforms) that the volunteer should follow after the meeting.

3. *Announce, don't argue.* The purpose of the meeting is simply, and only, to communicate to the volunteer that they are being separated from the agency. This meeting is not to re-discuss and re-argue the decision, because, if you followed the system, all the arguments have already been heard. You should also avoid arguing to make sure you don't put your foot in your mouth while venting your feelings. Expect the volunteer to vent, but keep yourself quiet. You must remain calm, no matter how ridiculous accusations against you become.

4. *Don't attempt to counsel.* If counseling were an option, you would not be having this meeting. Face reality; at this point you are not the friend of this former volunteer and any attempt to appear so is misguided and insulting.

5. *Follow-up.* Follow-up the meeting with a letter to the volunteer re-iterating the decision and informing them of any departure details. Make sure you also follow-up with others. Inform staff and clients of the change in status, although you do not need to inform them of the reasons behind the change. In particular, make sure that clients with a long relationship with

the volunteer are informed of the new volunteer to whom they are assigned.

Conclusion

While the above situations are extreme, they do exist, as you can determine by attending any DOVIA meeting. Volunteers are not necessarily better, or worse, than most other humans. As a volunteer manager you will sometimes need to take extreme steps to deal with extreme situations. The good news is that this will be a rare occurrence.

Chapter Six
Sample Volunteer Policies

The following are excerpted from *Volunteer Management: Mobilizing All the Resources of Your Community*, by Steve McCurley and Rick Lynch. They do not constitute a complete set of volunteer policies, but are samples of some policies which relate directly to handling problem volunteer situations.

Service at the discretion of the organization
The organization accepts the service of all volunteers with the understanding that such service is at the sole discretion of the organization. Volunteers agree that the organization may at any time, for whatever reason, decide to terminate the volunteer's relationship with the organization or to make changes in the nature of their volunteer assignment.

A volunteer may at any time, for whatever reason, decide to sever the volunteer's relationship with the organization. Notice of such a decision should be communicated as soon as possible to the volunteer's supervisor.

Maintenance of records
A system of records will be maintained on each volunteer, including dates of service, positions held, duties performed, evaluation of work, and awards received. Volunteers and appropriate staff shall be responsible for submitting all appropriate records and information to the volunteer management department in a timely and accurate fashion.

Volunteer personnel records shall be accorded the same confidentiality as staff personnel records.

Two hat policy
Members of the organization's board are [are not] accepted as direct service volunteers with the organization.

Conflict of interest
No person who has a conflict of interest with any activity or program of the organization, whether personal, philosophical, or financial shall be accepted or serve as a volunteer. Those volunteers who find themselves to be in a conflict situation should immediately report the nature of the conflict to their immediate supervisor.

Representation of the organization
Prior to any action or statement which might significantly affect or obligate the organization, volunteers should seek prior consultation and approval from appropriate staff. These actions may include, but are not limited to, public statements to the press, lobbying efforts with other organizations, collaborations or joint initiatives, or any agreements involving contractual or other financial obligations. Volunteers are authorized to act as representatives of the organization as specifically indicated within their job descriptions and only to the extent of such written specifications.

Confidentiality
Volunteers are responsible for maintaining the confidentiality of all proprietary or privileged information to which they are exposed while serving as a volunteer, whether this information involves a single member of staff, volunteer, client, or other person or involves the overall business of the organization.

Failure to maintain confidentiality may result in termination of the volunteer's relationship with the organization or other corrective action.

Dress code
As representatives of the organization, volunteers, like staff, are responsible for presenting a good image to clients and to the community. Volunteers shall dress appropriately for the conditions and performance of their duties.

Health screening
In cases where volunteers will be working with clients with health difficulties, a health screening procedure may be required prior to confirming the volunteer assignment. In addition, if there are physical requirements necessary for performance of a volunteer task, a screening or testing procedure may be required to ascertain the ability of the volunteer to safely perform that task.

Criminal records check
As appropriate for the protection of clients, volunteers in certain assignments may be asked to submit to a criminal record background check. Volunteers who do not agree to the background check may be refused assignment.

Placement with at-risk clients
Where volunteers are to be placed in direct contact with at-risk clients, additional screening procedures may be instituted. These pro-

Handling Problem Volunteers

cedures may include reference checks, direct background investigation, criminal investigation, etc. Volunteers who refuse permission for conduct of these checks will not be accepted for placement with clients.

Certificate of ability

Any potential volunteer who indicates that they are under the care of a doctor for either physical or psychological treatment may be asked to present a certificate from the doctor as to their ability to satis-factorily and safely perform their volunteer duties. Volunteers under a course of treatment which might affect their volunteer work will not be accepted without written verification of suitability from their doctor. Any volunteer who, after acceptance and assignment by the organization, enters a course of treatment which might adversely impact upon the performance of their volunteer duties should consult with the Volunteer Program Manager.

Falsification of Information

Falsification of information, including material omission or misrepresention, on a volunteer application is grounds for immediate dismissal.

Placement

In placing a volunteer in a position, attention shall be paid to the interests and capabilities of the volunteer and to the requirements of the volunteer position. No placement shall be made unless the requirements of both the volunteer and the supervising staff can be met: no volunteer should be assigned to a "make-work" position and no position should be given to an unqualified or uninterested volunteer.

Staff participation in interviewing and placement

Wherever possible, staff who will be working with the volunteer should participate in the design and conduct of the placement interview. Final assignment of a potential volunteer should not take place without the approval of appropriate staff with whom the volunteer will be working.

Acceptance and appointment

Service as a volunteer with the organization shall begin with an official notice of acceptance or appointment to a volunteer position. Notice may only be given by an authorized representative of the organization, who will normally be the Volunteer Program Manager. No volunteer shall begin performance of any position until

they have been officially accepted for that position and have completed all necessary screening and paperwork. At the time of final acceptance, each volunteer shall complete all necessary enrollment paperwork and shall receive a copy of their job description and agreement of service with the organization.

Probationary period

All volunteer placements shall initially be done on a trial period of 30 days. At the end of this period a second interview with the volunteer shall be conducted, at which point either the volunteer or staff may request a re-assignment of the volunteer to a different position or may determine the unsuitability of the volunteer for a position within the organization.

Re-assignment

Volunteers who are at any time re-assigned to a new position shall be interviewed for that position and shall receive all appropriate orientation and training for that position before they begin work. In addition, any screening procedures appropriate for that speci-fic position must be completed, even if the volunteer has already been working with the organization.

Length of service

All volunteer positions shall have a set term of duration. It is highly recommended that this term shall not be longer than one-year, with an option for renewal at the discretion of both parties. All volunteer assignments shall end at the conclusion of their set term, without expectation or requirement of re-assignment of that position to the incumbent.

Volunteers are neither expected nor required to continue their involvement with the organization at the end of their set term, although in most cases they are welcome to do so. They may instead seek a different volunteer assignment within the organization or with another organization, or may retire from volunteer service.

Leave of absence

At the discretion of the supervisor, leaves of absence may be granted to volunteers. This leave of absence will not alter or extend the previously agreed upon ending date of the volunteer's term of service. Volunteers are encouraged to seek leaves of absence when they need a break or are taking a vacation.

Requirement of a supervisor

Each volunteer who is accepted to a position with the organization must have a clearly identified supervisor who is responsible for direct management of that volunteer. This supervisor shall be responsible for day-to-day management and guidance of the work of the volunteer, and shall be available to the volunteer for consultation and assistance. The supervisor will have primary responsibility for developing suitable assignments for the volunteer, for involving the volunteer in the communication flow of the agency, and for providing feedback to the volunteer regarding their work. Staff who are assigned supervisory responsibility for volunteers shall have this responsibility delineated in their job descriptions.

Lines of communication

Volunteers are entitled to all necessary information pertinent to the performance of their work assignments. Accordingly, volunteers should be included in and have access to all appropriate information, memos, materials, meetings, and client records rele-vant to the work assignments. To facilitate the receipt of this information on a timely basis, volunteers should be included on all relevant distribution schedules and should be given a method for receipt of information circulated in their absence. Primary responsibility for ensuring that the volunteer receives such information will rest with the direct supervisor of the volunteer.

Lines of communication should operate in both directions, and should exist both formally and informally. Volunteers should be consulted regarding all decisions which would substantially affect the performance of their duties.

Absenteeism

Volunteers are expected to perform their duties on a regular scheduled and punctual basis. When expecting to be absent from a scheduled duty, volunteers should inform their staff supervisor as far in advance as possible so that alternative arrangements may be made. Continual absenteeism will result in a review of the volunteer's work assignment or term of service.

Sexual Harassment

A respectful work environment is essential to the well-being of both paid and unpaid employees. This agency does not condone or tolerate behavior which constitutes harassment in the workplace. Any unwarranted intrusion upon the sexual dignity of another which might be reasonably expected to cause offense, embarrassment or humiliation or which might be perceived as placing a condition of a sexual nature as a condition of work rights is strictly forbidden.

Standards of performance

Standards of performance shall be established for each volunteer position. These standards should list the work to be done in that position, measurable indicators of whether the work was accomplished to the required standards, and appropriate timeframes for accomplishment of the work. Creation of these standards will be a joint function of staff and the volunteer assigned to the position, and a copy of the standards should be provided to the volunteer along with a copy of their job description at the beginning of their assignment.

Evaluations

Volunteers shall receive periodic evaluation to review their work. The evaluation session will review the performance of the volunteer, suggest any changes in work style, seek suggestions from the volunteer on means of enhancing the volunteer's relationship with the organization, convey appreciation to the volunteer, and ascertain the continued interest of the volunteer in serving in that position. Evaluations should include both an examination of the volunteer's performance of his or her responsibi-lities and a discussion of any suggestions that the volunteer may have concerning the position or project with which the volunteer is connected.

The evaluation session is an opportunity for both the volunteer and the organization to examine and improve their relationship.

Written basis for evaluation

The position description and standards of performance for a volunteer position should form the basis of an evaluation. A written record should be kept of each evaluation session.

Staff responsibility for evaluation

It shall be the responsibility of each member of staff in a supervisory relationship with a volunteer to schedule and perform periodic evaluation and to maintain records of the evaluation.

Corrective action

In appropriate situations, corrective action may be taken following an evaluation. Examples of corrective action include the requirement for additional training, re-assignment of the volunteer to a new position, suspension of the volunteer, or dismissal from volunteer service.

Dismissal of a volunteer
Volunteers who do not adhere to the rules and procedures of the organization or who fail satisfactorily to perform their volunteer assignment may be subject to dismissal. No volunteer will be terminated until the volunteer has had an opportunity to discuss the reasons for possible dismissal with supervisory staff. Prior to dismissal of a volunteer, any affected member of staff should seek the consultation and assistance of the Volunteer Program Manager.

Reasons for dismissal
Possible grounds for dismissal may include, but are not limited to, the following: gross misconduct or insubordination, being under the influence of alcohol or drugs, theft of property or misuse of organization equipment or materials, abuse or mistreatment of clients or co-workers, failure to abide by organization policies and procedures, failure to meet physical or mental standards of performance, and failure satisfactorily to perform assigned duties.

Concerns and grievances
Decisions involving corrective action of a volunteer may be reviewed for appropriateness. If corrective action is taken, the affected volunteer shall be informed of the procedures for expressing their concern or grievance.

Notice of departure or re-assignment of a volunteer
In the event that a volunteer departs from the organization, whether voluntarily or involuntarily, or is re-assigned to a new position, it shall be the responsibi-lity of the volunteer management department to inform those affected staff and clients that the volunteer is no longer assigned to work with them. In cases of dismissal for good reason, this notification should be given in writing and should clearly indicate that any further contact with the volunteer must be outside the scope of any relationship with the organization.

Resignation
Volunteers may resign from their volunteer service with the organization at any time. It is requested that volunteers who intend to resign provide advance notice of their departure and a reason for their decision.

Exit interviews
Exit interviews, where possible, should be conducted with volunteers who are leaving their positions. The interview should ascertain why the volunteer is leaving the position, suggestions the volunteer may have to improving the position, and the possibility of involving the volunteer in some other capacity with the organization in the future.

Chapter Seven
Bibliography

ABA Center on Children and the Law, American Bar Association, *Criminal Record Checks: A Report for Nonprofits* (Washington, DC: The National Assembly) 1991.

Alessandra, Anthony, "Burnout: How You Can Try So Hard to Succeed and Yet Fail," *Voluntary Action Leadership*, Summer/Fall 1987.

Bailey, Mark, The Troublesome Board Member (Washington: National Center for Nonprofit Boards) 1996.

Beugen, Paula, "Supporting the Volunteer Life-Cycle," *Voluntary Action Leadership*, Fall 1985.

Branson, Floyd and Norman Long, "Dismissing a Volunteer," *Journal of Extension*, Winter 1992.

Camasso, Anne, "Myths about Low-Income Volunteers," *Journal of Extension*, March/April 1983.

Chambre, Susan, "Difficult Volunteers," *Volunteer Leadership*, Oct/Dec 1996.

Cook, Ann, "Retiring the Volunteer: Facing Reality when Service is No Longer Possible," *Journal of Volunteer Administration*, Summer 1992.

Corrigan, Marilyn, "Burnout: How to Spot It and Protect Yourself Against It," *Journal of Volunteer Administration*, Spring 1994.

Cyr, Carolyn and Peter Dowrick, "Burnout in Crisisline Volunteers," *Administration and Policy in Mental Health*, May 1991.

Dean, Laurel, "Learning about Volunteer Burnout," *Voluntary Action Leadership*, Winter 1985.

Disney, Diane, Sarah Jane Rehnborg, Laura Roberts, Julie Washburn, and Vanda Williamson, "Should Volunteers Be Fired: Several Considerations," *Voluntary Action Leadership*, Fall 1979.

Finn Paradis, L., L. Miller, and V. Runnion, "Volunteer Stress and Burnout: Issues for Administrators," *Hospice Journal*, Vol 3(2/3), 1987.

Gaston, Nancy, "Easy Does It: Initiating a Performance Evaluation Process in an Existing Volunteer Program," *Journal of Volunteer Administration*, Fall 1989.

Gaston, Nancy, "Everyone Can Win: Creative Resolution of Conflict," *Journal of Volunteer Administration*, Summer 1989.

Glass, Conrad, and Janice Hastings, "Stress and Burnout: Concerns for the Hospice Volunteer," *Educational Gerontologist*, Oct/Nov 1992.

Graff, Linda, *By Definition: Policies for Volunter Programs* (Etobicoke, ON: Volunteer Ontario) 1993.

Howell, Albert, *Why do Volunteers Burnout and Dropout?* (Calgary: Research Unit for Public Policy Studies, University of Calgary) December 1986.

Kessler, Marcia, "Preventing Burnout: Taking the Stress Out of the Job," *Journal of Volunteer Administration*, Spring 1991.

Keys, L.M. "Former Patients as Volunteers in Community Agencies: A Model Work Rehabilitation Program," *Hospital and Community Psychology*, December 1982.

Knowles, Don, "On the Tendency of Volunteer Helpers to Give Advice," *Journal of Counseling Psychology*, July 1979.

Lafta, Lorraine, "When to Say 'No' to an Interested Volunteer: The Screening Process," *Alcohol Health and Research World*, 1982 (3).

Lang, E. and A. Richman, "Project Outreach: Volunteer Transitional Employment," *Psychiatric Hospital*, Spring 1984.

Lundin, Shirley, "When All Else Fails: Releasing a Volunteer," *Journal of Volunteer Administration*, Fall 1996.

Lynch, Rick, *Precision Management* (Seattle: Abbot Press) 1988.

Lynch Rick and Sue Vineyard, *Secrets of Leadership* (Downers Grove: Heritage Arts) 1991.

Handling Problem Volunteers

Lynott, Nancy and Ann Narkiewicz, "Termination Techniques: Ending the Volunteer/Client Relationship," *Journal of Volunteer Administration*, Spring 1990.

Macduff, Nancy, and Janie Millgard, "Managing Conflict," *Voluntary Action Leadership*, Summer 1989.

MacKenzie, M., *Dealing with Difficult Volunteers*, (Downers Grove: Heritage Arts) 1988.

McCurley, Steve and Rick Lynch, *Volunteer Management: Mobilizing All the Resources of the Community* (Downers Grove: Heritage Arts) 1996.

McCurley, Steve and Sue Vineyard, *Measuring Up: Assessment Tools for Volunteer Programs*, (Downers Grove: Heritage Arts) 1997.

McCurley, Steve, "A Guide to Leading Your Former Peers," *Grapevine*, Nov/Dec 1996.

McCurley, Steve, "Evaluating Volunteers," *Grapevine*, March/April 1995.

McCurley, Steve, "How the 'New' Volunteers Will Change Volunteer Management," *Grapevine*, Sept/Oct 1997.

McCurley, Steve, "How to Fire a Volunteer and Live to Tell About It," *Grapevine*, January/February 1993.

O'Neill, Barbara, "How to Avoid 'Firing' Your Volunteers," *Journal of Extension*, Fall 1990.

Paradis, L.F., B. Miller, and V.M. Runnion, "Volunteer Stress and Burnout: Issues for Administrators," *Hospital Journal*, Summer/Fall 1987.

Park, Jane Mallory, "The Fourth R: A Case for Releasing Volunteers," *Journal of Volunteer Administration*, Spring 1984.

Raymond, Bruce, "Do It My Way, or Get Someone Else," *Canadian Fundraiser*, February 26, 1997.

Raymond, Bruce, "Handling the Temperamental Prima Donna," *Canadian Fundraiser*, March 12, 1997.

Schumann, Ginnie, "The Transitional Volunteer," *Journal of Volunteer Administration*, Spring 1987.

Scribner, Susan, Boards from Hell (Long Beach: Scribner & Associates) 1991.

Thomason, Deborah, "Conflict: What It is and How It Can be Managed," *Journal of Volunteer Administration*, Spring 1997.

Thornburg, Linda, "Evaluating Volunteers for Positive Results," *Voluntary Action Leadership*, Fall 1992.

Vineyard, Sue, *Evaluating Volunteers, Programs and Events* (Downers Grove: Heritage Arts) 1988.

Vineyard, Sue, *How to Take Care of You...So You Can Take Care of Others* (Downers Grove: Heritage Arts) 1987.

Vineyard, Sue, *Secrets of Motivation: How to Get and Keep Volunteers and Staff*, (Downers Grove: Heritage Arts) 1990.

Weaver, John, *An Untapped Resource: Working with Volunteers Who are Mentally Ill* (Walla Walla: MBA Publishing) 1993.

Yarbrough, Elaine, *Constructive Conflict* (Downers Grove: Heritage Arts) 1988.

About the Authors

Sue Vineyard

Sue Vineyard is a partner in VMSystems and the President of Heritage Arts Publishing. From 1973-1979 she worked with Project Concern International, a charity which annually serves over a million children of poverty worldwide. Rising to National Director, she worked with over 30,000 volunteers raising pledges of $17 million across the nation.

Sue is the author of 14 best-selling books for volunteer leaders and is the editor of the highly acclaimed newsletter *Grapevine*, which links people in volunteer involvement across America. She is a nationally-acclaimed trainer and consultant in volunteer management.

Sue is the receipient of many awards for her work in human services, including "Outstanding Young Women of America," in 1974, and the "Distinguished Service Award" of the Association for Volunteer Administration in 1986.

She lives in Downers Grove, IL.

Steve McCurley

Steve McCurley is an internationally-known trainer and speaker in the field of effective volunteer involvement.

At the national level, Steve has provided consulting services on volunteer involvement to groups such as AARP, Special Olympics International, the National Park Service, the Points of Light Foundation, and many others. Each year he gives workshops to over 15,000 participants from groups as diverse as the American Hospital Association, the Fraternal Congress of America, the Nature Conservancy, and Samsung, Inc. He is the author of 12 books and more than 100 articles on volunteer management, including the bestselling basic text, *Volunteer Management*.

On the international front, Steve has done work in Canada, England, the Caribbean, and South America. His writings have been translated into Spanish, Portuguese, Russian, Hebrew, and Korean, among other languages.

Steve lives in Olympia, WA.